Looney Tun COLLECTIBLES

An Unauthorized Guide

Debra S. Braun

Schiffer Publishing Ltd ®

4880 Lower Valley Road, Atglen, PA 19310 USA

Disclaimer

Looney Tunes ™ and Merrie Melodies ™ are registered trademarks of Warner Bros. All pictures, graphics, and photos compiled herein are intended to heighten the awareness of Looney Tunes ™, Merrie Melodies ™, and related products. This book is in no way intended to infringe on the intellectual property rights of any party. All products, brands, characters, and names represented are trademarks or registered trademarks of their respective companies.

The information in this book is derived from the author's independent research and is not authorized, furnished, or approved by Warner Bros.

Opposite page: Collector plate, ceramic. Manufacturer unknown, 1995. Limited edition of 2,500 pieces. This was the third plate in the series. Sketches of Pepé Le Pew and Penelope are shown. For decorative use only. 10.25" in diameter. $45-60. TM & © Warner Bros. Inc.

Copyright page: Candy container, plastic. Ullman Co., 1995. Heart shaped container with Bugs Bunny and friends on the cover. 5.5" tall. $5-10. TM & © Warner Bros. Inc.

Title page:
Left: Serving tray, metal. Manufacturer unknown, 1974. The tray depicts Bugs Bunny and friends. 11.75" in diameter. $20-35. TM & © Warner Bros. Inc.

Top right: Figurine, plastic. Kinder, 1997. Germany. Speedy Gonzales is shown holding a chunk of cheese. 1.75" tall. $10-15. TM & © Warner Bros. Inc.

Bottom center: Doll, vinyl. Manufacturer unknown, 1995. "Looney Tunes classic original collector doll" series. K-9. 7.5" tall. $20-35. TM & © Warner Bros. Inc.

Copyright © 1999 by Debra S. Braun
Library of Congress Catalog Card Number: 98-83099

Designed by Bonnie M. Hensley
Type set in Brush455 BT/Souvenir Lt BT

ISBN: 0-7643-0823-8
Printed in China
1 2 3 4

Dedication

This book is dedicated to all of the Looney Tunes ™ fans that are patiently waiting for Wile E. Coyote to catch the Road Runner.

Published by Schiffer Publishing Ltd.
4880 Lower Valley Road
Atglen, PA 19310
Phone: (610) 593-1777; Fax: (610) 593-2002
E-mail: Schifferbk@aol.com
Please visit our web site catalog at
www.schifferbooks.com

This book may be purchased from the publisher.
Include $3.95 for shipping. Please try your bookstore first.
We are interested in hearing from authors
with book ideas on related subjects.
You may write for a free printed catalog.

In Europe, Schiffer books are distributed by
Bushwood Books
6 Marksbury Avenue
Kew Gardens
Surrey TW9 4JF England
Phone: 44 (0)181 392-8585; Fax: 44 (0)181 392-9876
E-mail: Bushwd@aol.com

Contents

Acknowledgments

I would like to extend a special thanks to my parents, Mark Coté, Peter and Nancy Schiffer, Jennifer Lindbeck, Tracey Curry, and the staff at Wink One Hour Photo. All of these people were instrumental in the development of this book. I really appreciate all of their guidance and support.

I would also like to thank my co-workers and friends for believing in me and making me smile.

Figurine, rubber. Tyco Playtime, Inc., 1993. Bendable. Taz. 5" tall. $15-20. TM & © Warner Bros. Inc.

Introduction

In the early 1900s, Sam Warner was shown Thomas Edison's invention the "kinetoscope." It was used to view motion picture filmstrips. Sam was so intrigued that he took a job as a projectionist. He found inspiration in the film industry and persuaded his three brothers to enter the field. Each of them had diverse backgrounds and were able to make effective contributions toward building a movie empire. In 1925, their dreams came to fruition, when they acquired the Vitagraph Co., Stanley Theatres, and First National Pictures.

The "vitagraph" is an invention that enables pre-recorded sound to be correlated with cartoons and motion picture films. Introduced into the marketplace in 1926, this novel device enabled Warner Bros. to gain a competitive advantage. Eventually, Warner Bros. entered a partnership with Western Electric, a merger that became known as the Vitaphone Corp.

Economically, the people of the 1930s were hit hard by the Depression Era. Audiences were looking for excitement and escape at the movies. A standard movie fare usually included a cartoon, news reel, or travelogue along with the feature presentation. In 1930, Warner Bros. debuted their first Looney Tunes animated series during their *Vitaphone Shorts*. This popular series revolved around a cartoon character named "Bosko." In 1931, the Merrie Melodies characters evolved from the Looney Tunes series. They were another animated series designed to promote Warner Bros. music releases. Composer Carl Stalling is famous for converting samples of folk and classical music from the Warner Bros. catalog into over 600 cartoon scores.

At the onset of World War II, Warner Bros. created Bugs Bunny to represent the role America played in the war. Born in 1940, his character is most noted for the strong displays of patriotism in defense of his homeland. Bugs Bunny was so well received that audiences couldn't get enough of him. In addition to cartoon clips, Bugs Bunny was featured in two movies with Jack Carson, *Two Guys from Texas* and *My Dream is Yours*. These two films mark the first time that a cartoon character was transitioned into feature films.

Warner Bros. continued to enjoy success and stability decade after decade. They expanded considerably from their humble beginnings and were able to recruit choice staff members along the way. Veteran animators like Tex Avery, Bill Clampett, Friz Freleng, Chuck Jones, Robert McKimson, and Virgil Ross gave life to one classic character after another. Dynamic narrators like Mel Blanc, Arthur Q. Bryan, and Joe Dougherty gave each character its own heart and soul. Another key player in the production was Tregoweth "Treg" Brown. He engineered all of the special "boink-zoink" type of sound effects associated with each cartoon.

Below is a brief outline of the date each character debuted:

Bugs Bunny - Merrie Melodies, *A Wild Hare.* (1940)
Daffy Duck - Looney Tunes, *Porky's Duck Hunt.* (1937)
Elmer Fudd - Merrie Melodies, *A Wild Hare.* (1940)
Foghorn Leghorn - Merrie Melodies, *Wally Talky Hawky.* (1946)
Granny - Merrie Melodies, *Canary Row.* (1950)
Marvin the Martian - Looney Tunes, *Haredevil Hare.* (1948)
Michigan J. Frog - Merrie Melodies, *One Froggy Evening.* (1955)
Pepé Le Pew - Looney Tunes, *Odor-able Kitty.* (1945)
Porky Pig - Merrie Melodies, *I Haven't Got a Hat.* (1935)
Road Runner - Looney Tunes, *Fast and Furry-ous.* (1949)
Speedy Gonzales - Merrie Melodies, *Cat-Tails for Two.* (1953)
Sylvester - Merrie Melodies, *Life with Feathers.* (1945)
Sylvester Jr. - Looney Tunes, *Pop 'Im, Pop!* (1950)
Tasmanian Devil - Looney Tunes, *Devil May Hare.* (1954)
Tweety - Merrie Melodies, *Birdy and the Beast.* (1944) (It's interesting to note that the phrase "I tawt I taw a puddy tat" was coined in Merrie Melodies *A Tale of Two Kitties (1942)*. This was approximately *two* years before Tweety debuted.)
Wile E. Coyote - Looney Tunes, *Fast and Furry-ous.* (1949)
Yosemite Sam - Merrie Melodies, *Hare Trigger.* (1945)

Out of all the characters mentioned, Bugs Bunny is one of the most adored. Even after almost 60 years, he is still an American icon. This could be attributed to the fact that he was concocted from a "melting pot" of many legendary animators.

In 1960, Bugs Bunny was given his own television show on primetime ABC, and, in 1989, he was awarded a star on the prestigious "Hollywood Boulevard-Hollywood Walk of Fame."

In 1990, he turned 50 (He's one grey "hare" that none of us mind!), and, in 1997, he was the first Looney Tunes character to be put on a United States of America postage stamp. ***You don't need to eat carrots to see what's up . . . it's the popularity of Looney Tunes, Doc!***

If you would like to receive a Looney Tunes merchandising catalog, the phone number for the Warner Bros. Studio Store is 1-800-223-6524 or the website address is: http://wbstore.com

Mug, ceramic. Matrix Industries, Ltd., 1997. Sylvester is shown with snowflakes in the background. 4" tall. $5-10. TM & © Warner Bros. Inc.

Helpful Hints

Searching for Looney Tunes ™ items at toy shows, flea markets, and garage sales is challenging and fun. You never know what you are going to find. It is important to understand that the prices for Looney Tunes ™ memorabilia will fluctuate according to their condition, supply, and demand. You should purchase an object because you like it, not as an investment. This book is intended to heighten your awareness of Looney Tunes ™ collectibles and their approximate values in excellent to mint condition on a secondary market. All the items shown in this book were produced on or before 1998.

There are several things to consider before purchasing an object. For example: Is it in good condition? Are all of the pieces complete? Is it rare and hard to find? It is my recommendation to inspect each item thoroughly. Especially look for chips, hairline cracks, paint peeling, and crazing on ceramic items.

Tip 1

One way to identify a hairline crack in an object is to hold it up to a light. The hairline crack should stick out instantly even if it has been repaired.

Tip 2

To feel a chip easily, gently move your finger around the entire surface of an object.

Tip 3

Price tags sometimes get so sticky that they can ruin any object. If you are considering a purchase, you may want to ask the vendor to carefully remove his price tag so that the exact condition is disclosed.

Tip 4

Sunlight can cause **permanent** discoloration on plastic or plush materials if an object is exposed over a significant period of time.

Tip 5

If an item is made up of multiple parts, take the time to make sure that all pieces are accounted for. There is nothing more disappointing then putting together a puzzle that has pieces missing.

Tip 6

Before you purchase a battery operated toy, check inside the battery compartment for corrosion. Also, you may want to carry an assortment of batteries to make sure the toy works.

Keep in mind that if a slight imperfection is in an inconspicuous place, then the object may still look nice on a display.

Most of us are on a budget, so every penny counts. Once you have established what type of condition the object is in, you should also estimate a fair price. I usually rate the object first on rarity, then on condition. If an object is rare, I would probably buy it at any price even with slight imperfections. However, if an object is common, I may wait until I can find it somewhere in mint condition.

I estimate the condition of an object on a scale from 1 to 10 and price it accordingly.

Grade	Condition	Definition	Price example
1-4	Poor	Item shows major signs of wear. No tags and/or packaging present, i.e., noticeably broken, reglued, or discolored.	$1.00 - $4.00
5	Fair	Item shows minor signs of wear and has some missing components. No tags and/or packaging present, i.e., missing puzzle or game pieces.	$5.00
6	Good	Item has been used and shows minor signs of wear. No tags and/or packaging present, i.e., small chip in an inconspicuous area or very slight crazing.	$6.00
7	Very Good	Item has been used but is still pristine. No tags and/or packaging present.	$7.00
8	Excellent	Item has been gently used but is still pristine. Original tags and/or packaging may be ripped or damaged.	$8.00
9	Near mint	Item has been gently used but is still pristine. Original tags and/or packaging may be unsealed and slightly worn.	$9.00
10	Mint	Item has never been used and is pristine. Original tags are present and/or packaging is sealed from the factory.	$10.00

One last thing, vendors at flea markets and toy shows **expect** you to barter on prices. Don't be shy! If an object is priced too expensive for the condition that it is in, let the vendor know in a diplomatic manner. If your criticism is warranted, the vendor will often reduce his asking price. Best of luck in your hunting endeavors!

Nodder statue, resin. Manufacturer unknown, 1996. Road Runner is shown eating free bird seed. Wile E. Coyote is shown with an anvil on his head. 9.5" tall. $125-140. TM & © Warner Bros. Inc.

Figurines

Figurine, plastic. Kinder, N/A. Germany. Figurines were placed sparatically within chocolate eggs. Speedy Gonzales. 1.25" tall. $15-20. TM & © Warner Bros. Inc.

Author's note: *Kinder figurines are finely engineered. They are made up of small pieces which are put together like a puzzle. Early figurines have sticker eyes and accents; while later ones have painted features.*

Figurine, plastic. Kinder, 1997. Germany. Road Runner is shown with a pile of bird seed. 2.75" tall. $15-20. TM & © Warner Bros. Inc.

Figurine, plastic. Kinder, 1997. Germany. Wile E. Coyote is shown with a detonator. 2.5" tall. $10-15. TM & © Warner Bros. Inc.

Figurine, plastic. Kinder, 1997. Germany. Sylvester is shown with a fly swatter. 1.75" tall. $10-15. TM & © Warner Bros. Inc.

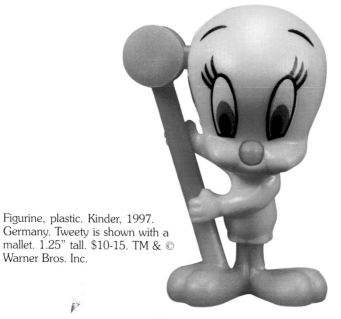

Figurine, plastic. Kinder, 1997. Germany. Tweety is shown with a mallet. 1.25" tall. $10-15. TM & © Warner Bros. Inc.

Figurine, plastic. Kinder, 1997. Germany. Speedy Gonzales is shown holding a chunk of cheese. 1.75" tall. $10-15. TM & © Warner Bros. Inc.

Figurine, plastic. Kinder, 1997. Germany. Daffy Duck. 1.75" tall. $10-15. TM & © Warner Bros. Inc.

Figurine, plastic. Kinder, 1997. Germany. Elmer Fudd is shown wearing his hunting attire. 2" tall. $10-15. TM & © Warner Bros. Inc.

Figurine, plastic. Kinder, 1997. Germany. Bugs Bunny is shown wearing a holster with carrots. 2.75" tall. $10-15. TM & © Warner Bros. Inc.

Figurine, plastic. R. Dakin & Co., N/A. Porky Pig is wearing a polka dot tie. 4" tall. $20-35. TM & © Warner Bros. Inc.

Figurines, ceramic. Manufacturer unknown, 1998. Daffy Duck, Foghorn Leghorn, and Taz. Approximately 1.75" tall. $10-15 each. TM & © Warner Bros. Inc.

Figurines, ceramic. Manufacturer unknown, 1998. Elmer Fudd, Petunia, and Porky Pig. Approximately 1.75" tall. $10-15 each. TM & © Warner Bros. Inc.

Figurines, ceramic. Manufacturer unknown, 1998. Yosemite Sam, Marc Antony, and Pepé Le Putois. Approximately 1.75" tall. $10-15 each. TM & © Warner Bros. Inc.

Figurines, ceramic. Manufacturer unknown, 1998. Bugs Bunny (standing), Bugs Bunny (laying down), and Lola Bunny. Approximately 1.75" tall. $10-15 each. TM & © Warner Bros. Inc.

Figurines, plastic. Arby's promotion, 1987. "Looney Tunes on Oval Bases" series. Complete set of seven. Pepé Le Pew, Yosemite Sam, and Porky Pig. Approximately 2" tall. $10-15 each. TM & © Warner Bros. Inc.

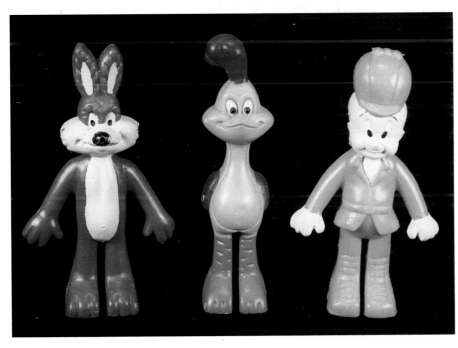

Figurines, plastic. Arby's promotion, 1988. "Looney Tunes Straight Legged Characters" series. Complete set of six. Wile E. Coyote, Road Runner, and Elmer Fudd. Approximately 3" tall. $5-10 each. TM & © Warner Bros. Inc.

Figurines 13

Figurines, plastic. Arby's promotion, 1989. "Looney Tunes Fun Figures" series. Complete set of three. Titled "Freshman Daffy" and "Fireman Sylvester." Approximately 2.25" tall. $10-15 each. TM & © Warner Bros. Inc.

Figurine, plastic. Applause, Inc., 1990. Official licensee Major League Baseball. First series. Complete set of 18. Sylvester is dressed in a St. Louis Cardinals uniform. 2.5" tall. $10-15. TM & © Warner Bros. Inc.

Figurine, plastic. Applause, Inc., 1990. Official licensee Major League Baseball. First series. Complete set of 18. Porky Pig is dressed in a Houston Astros uniform. 2.5" tall. $10-15. TM & © Warner Bros. Inc.

Figurine, plastic. Applause, Inc., 1990. Official licensee Major League Baseball. First series. Complete set of 18. Tweety is dressed in a Philadelphia Phillies uniform. 3" tall. $10-15. TM & © Warner Bros. Inc.

Applause, Inc., 1994. Marvin the Martian is shown in his space ship. Caption: "Have an earth-shattering birthday!" 2" tall. $10-15. TM & © Warner Bros. Inc.

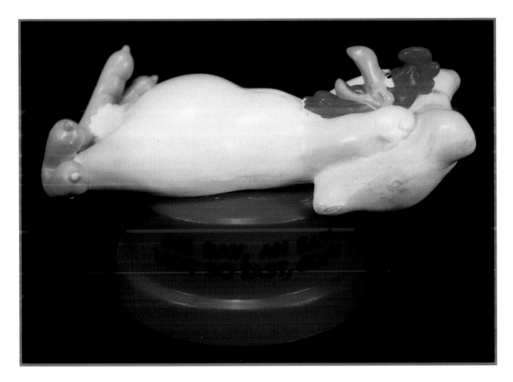

Figurine, plastic. Applause, Inc., 1994. Foghorn Leghorn is shown laying on a pillow. Caption: "Ah say, ah say, not so fast, son!" 1.75" tall. $10-15. TM & © Warner Bros. Inc.

Figurine, plastic. Applause, Inc., 1997. Tweety is shown in the bath tub. The base is in the shape of a film reel. Caption: *"Tweet and Lovely.* 1959. Friz Freleng." 2" tall. $10-15. TM & © Warner Bros. Inc.

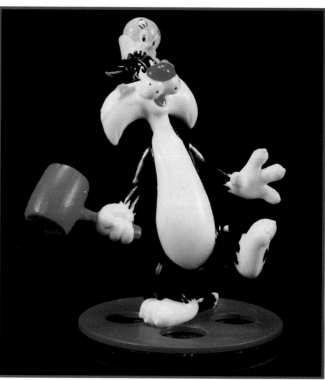

Figurine, plastic. Applause, Inc., 1997. Sylvester is shown holding a mallet. The base is in the shape of a film reel. Caption: *"Home Tweet Home.* 1950. Friz Freleng." 3.5" tall. $10-15. TM & © Warner Bros. Inc.

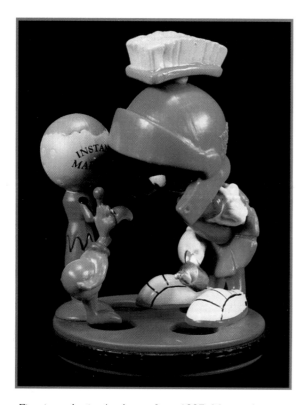

Figurine, plastic. Applause, Inc., 1997. Marvin the Martian is shown with an instant Martian machine. The base is in the shape of a film reel. Caption: *"Hare-way to the Stars.* 1958. Charles M. Jones." 3" tall. $10-15. TM & © Warner Bros. Inc.

Figurine, plastic. Applause, Inc., 1997. Bugs Bunny is shown with Gossamer. The base is in the shape of a film reel. Caption: *"Water, Water Every Hare.* 1952. Charles M. Jones." 3.5" tall. $10-15. TM & © Warner Bros. Inc.

Figurine, rubber. Tyco Playtime, Inc., 1993. Bendable. Taz. 5" tall. $15-20. TM & © Warner Bros. Inc.

Figurine, rubber. Tyco Playtime, Inc., 1993. Bendable. Bugs Bunny. 6.5" tall. $15-20. TM & © Warner Bros. Inc.

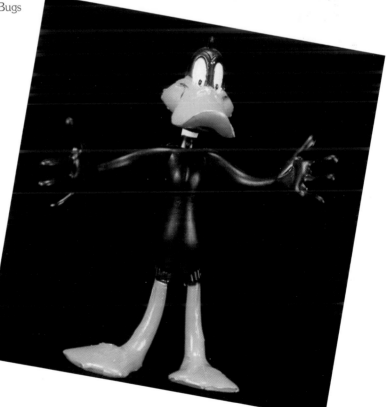

Figurine, rubber. Tyco Playtime, Inc., 1993. Bendable. Daffy Duck. 6" tall. $15-20. TM & © Warner Bros. Inc.

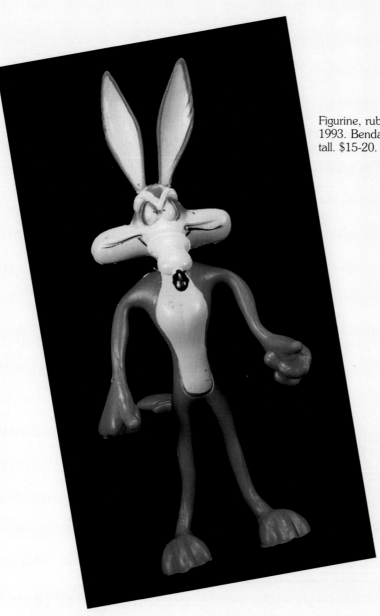

Figurine, rubber. Tyco Playtime, Inc.,
1993. Bendable. Wile E. Coyote. 7.5"
tall. $15-20. TM & © Warner Bros. Inc.

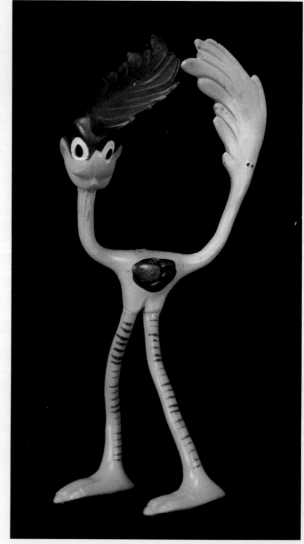

Figurine, rubber. Manufacturer unknown,
1978. Bendable. Road Runner. 6.25" tall.
$20-35. TM & © Warner Bros. Inc.

Kitchen

Teapot, ceramic. Manufacturer unknown, 1997. Sylvester is shown peeking out of a blue teapot. 10" tall. $60-75. TM & © Warner Bros. Inc.

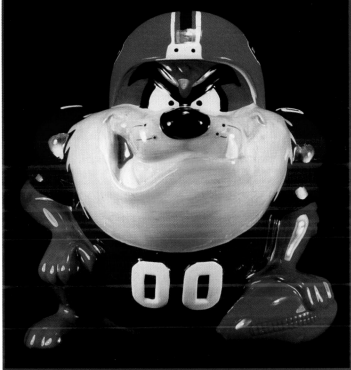

Cookie jar, ceramic. Certified International Corp., 1994. Taz is dressed in a Buffalo Bills football uniform. 9.5" tall. $50-65. TM & © Warner Bros. Inc.

Cookie jar, ceramic. Manufacturer unknown, 1996. Pepé Le Pew is shown with Penelope. 12.5" tall. $150-165. TM & © Warner Bros. Inc.

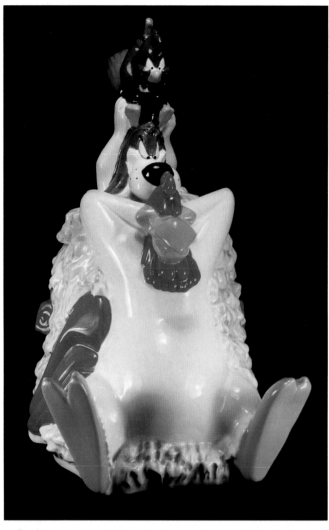

Cookie jar, ceramic. Manufacturer unknown, 1996. Foghorn Leghorn is shown sleeping against a pile of hay. 13.5" tall. $150-165. TM & © Warner Bros. Inc.

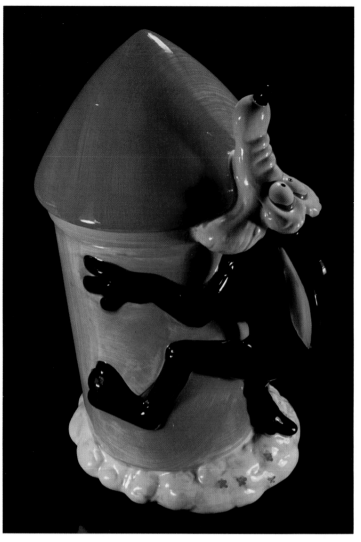

Cookie jar, ceramic. Certified International Corp., 1993. Wile E. Coyote is shown on the side of a rocket. 12" tall. $85-100. TM & © Warner Bros. Inc.

Canister set, tin. Manufacturer unknown, 1994. When the four canisters are assembled, "Downtown Looneyville" is formed. Under 15" tall. $50-65 set. TM & © Warner Bros. Inc.

Salt and pepper shakers, ceramic. Certified International Corp., 1993. Taz is dressed as a football player. Bugs Bunny is dressed as a referee. Taz: 3" tall. Bugs Bunny: 5.25" tall. $20-35 set. TM & © Warner Bros. Inc.

Salt and pepper shakers, ceramic. Certified International Corp., 1993. Bugs Bunny and Yosemite Sam are dressed in their western attire. Bugs Bunny: 5.25" tall. Yosemite Sam: 3.75" tall. $20-35 set. TM & © Warner Bros. Inc.

Salt and pepper shakers, ceramic. Certified International Corp., 1993. Bugs Bunny is holding a "Duck season" sign. Elmer Fudd is shown wearing a hunting outfit. Bugs Bunny: 5.25" tall. Elmer Fudd: 4.75" tall. $20-35 set. TM & © Warner Bros. Inc.

Salt and pepper shakers, ceramic. Certified International Corp., 1993. Wile E. Coyote and Road Runner are shown hiding behind cactuses. Wile E. Coyote: 5.5" tall. Road Runner: 4.75" tall. $25-40 set. TM & © Warner Bros. Inc.

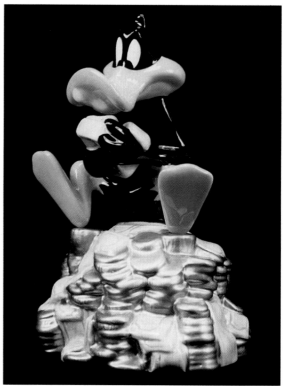

Salt and pepper shakers, ceramic. Manufacturer unknown, 1996. Daffy Duck is shown sitting on a pile of money. Daffy Duck: 3.5" tall. Pile of money: 2.5" tall. $20-35 set. TM & © Warner Bros. Inc.

Salt and pepper shakers, ceramic. Manufacturer unknown, 1996. Wile E. Coyote is shown squashed under an "ACME" anvil. Wile E. Coyote: 2.25" tall. Anvil: 2.75" tall. $20-35 set. TM & © Warner Bros. Inc.

Salt and pepper shakers, ceramic. Manufacturer unknown, 1997. Sylvester is trying to make a Tweety sandwich. Sylvester: 4" tall. Tweety: 3.5" tall. $20-35 set. TM & © Warner Bros. Inc.

Salt and pepper shakers, ceramic. Manufacturer unknown, 1997. Pepé Le Pew and Penelope interlock. Pepé Le Pew: 3.5" tall. Penelope: 3.5" tall. $25-40 set. TM & © Warner Bros. Inc.

Plate, ceramic. Manufacturer unknown, 1992. Bugs Bunny is shown with a green zig-zag border. Caption: "What's up, Doc? This "Hare-Extra" extraordinare can handle any situation without losing his grip on his carrot. He's an international star and the King of cool." Various characters adorned matching place settings and kitchen accessories. Mix and match. 8" in diameter. $20-35. TM & © Warner Bros. Inc.

Plate, ceramic. Manufacturer unknown, 1992. Pepé Le Pew is shown with a blue and white striped border. Caption: "Come wiz me and we will make zee love tu jour a moor." Various characters adorned matching place settings and kitchen accessories. Mix and match. 8" in diameter. $25-40. TM & © Warner Bros. Inc.

Plate, ceramic. Manufacturer unknown, 1992. Road Runner is shown with a red and blue plaid border. Caption: "Beep Beep. Road Runner debuted in 1949 in *Fast and Furryous*, and has been giving Wile E. Coyote the runaround *ever since*." Various characters adorned matching place settings and kitchen accessories. Mix and match. 8" in diameter. $25-40. TM & © Warner Bros. Inc.

Plate, ceramic. Manufacturer unknown, 1992. Taz is shown with a maroon and white polka dot border. Caption: "@ #!?%!!! The original party animal: He's a slobbering, snarling tornado with an appetite for destruction and food." Various characters adorned matching place settings and kitchen accessories. Mix and match. 8" in diameter. $20-35. TM & © Warner Bros. Inc.

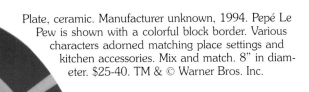

Plate, ceramic. Manufacturer unknown, 1994. Pepé Le Pew is shown with a colorful block border. Various characters adorned matching place settings and kitchen accessories. Mix and match. 8" in diameter. $25-40. TM & © Warner Bros. Inc.

Plate, ceramic. Manufacturer unknown, 1994. Bugs Bunny and friends are shown in a soda shop. Caption: "Drive in or drop by luncheonette." Various characters adorned matching place settings and kitchen accessories. Mix and match. This also came in light green. 8" in diameter. $15-20. TM & © Warner Bros. Inc.

Plate, ceramic. Manufacturer unknown, 1994. Foghorn Leghorn is shown outside a Dairy. Caption: "NYC Delancey Street." Various characters adorned matching place settings and kitchen accessories. Mix and match. 10.5" in diameter. $15-20. TM & © Warner Bros. Inc.

Dinnerware set, plastic. Zak designs, 1992. Bugs Bunny, Daffy Duck, and Marvin the Martian decorate each piece with a space theme. Set includes one plate, bowl, and cup. One size. $20-35 set. TM & © Warner Bros. Inc.

Silverware. Manufacturer unknown, 1975. Tweety and Sylvester are shown on the handles of stainless steel spoons. 5.5" tall. $10-15 each. TM & © Warner Bros. Inc.

Silverware. Gift Creations, Inc., 1991. Road Runner and Sylvester are shown on the handles of silver plated spoons. 4.75" tall. $15-20 each. TM & © Warner Bros. Inc.

Utensil holder, ceramic. Manufacturer unknown, 1995. Pepé Le Pew is shown holding a blue bag. 8" tall. $35-50. TM & © Warner Bros. Inc.

Placemat, plastic. Pepsi promotion, 1976. Sylvester is shown flying with a bunch of balloons tied around his waist while Tweety is trying to pop them. 10.5" tall. $10-15. TM & © Warner Bros. Inc.

Placemat, plastic. Pepsi promotion, 1976. Wile E. Coyote is shown placing dynamite on the road while Road Runner is throwing a rock down on the detonator. 10.5" tall. $15-20. TM & © Warner Bros. Inc.

Placemat, plastic. Pepsi promotion, 1976. Bugs Bunny and Elmer Fudd are shown surfing. 10.5" tall. $10-15. TM & © Warner Bros. Inc.

Kitchen 27

Serving tray, metal. Manufacturer unknown, 1974. The tray depicts Bugs Bunny and friends. 11.75" in diameter. $20-35. TM & © Warner Bros. Inc.

Bowl, plastic. Manufacturer unknown, 1996. Bugs Bunny and friends decorate the center and edge of the bowl. Caption: "Happy Easter." 14.5" in diameter. $5-10. TM & © Warner Bros. Inc.

Candy dish, ceramic. Manufacturer unknown, 1997. Tweety is shown sitting on some Easter eggs. 4" tall. $30-45. TM & © Warner Bros. Inc.

Bags. Fun Designs, Inc., 1997. "Zipper Sandwich & Storage Bags." Two different designs. 6.5" tall. $5-10. TM & © Warner Bros. Inc.

Center piece, paper/tissue. Reeds, 1977. Bugs Bunny & friends surround an oversized carrot. 14.5" tall. $40-55. TM & © Warner Bros. Inc.

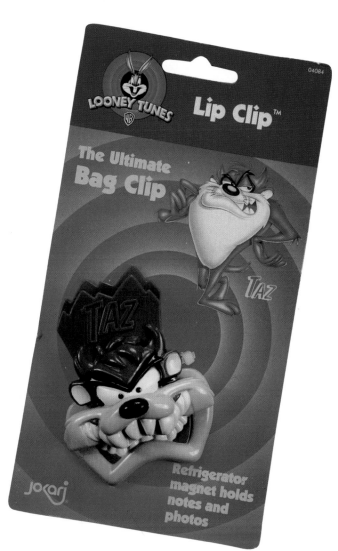

Bag clip, plastic. Jokari/US, Inc., 1997. Various characters were produced. Taz's head. 3.25" tall. $5-10. TM & © Warner Bros. Inc.

Cap, plastic. Jokari/US, Inc., 1994. "Fizz-keeper Pump Cap." The cap is used to keep soda carbonated. Various characters were produced. Bugs Bunny. 5.5" tall. $5-10. TM & © Warner Bros. Inc.

Magnet, coated paper. Manufacturer unknown, 1993. Titled *"Bugs Bunny in A Witch's Tangled Hare."* 2.25" tall. $5-10. TM & © Warner Bros. Inc.

Magnet, coated paper. Manufacturer unknown, 1993. Titled *"Tweety and Sylvester in Muzzle Tough."* 2.25" tall. $5-10. TM & © Warner Bros. Inc.

Magnet, plastic. Applause, Inc., 1988. Wile E. Coyote is shown on a rocket. 1.75" tall. $10-15. TM & © Warner Bros. Inc.

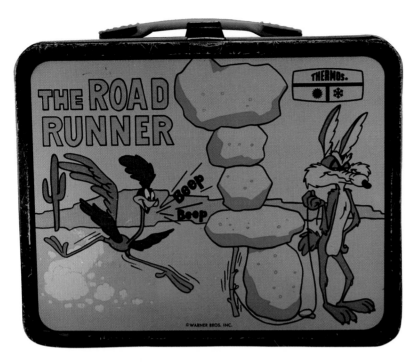

Lunch box, metal. Thermos Company, 1970. Wile E. Coyote and Road Runner are shown in the desert. 7" tall. $75-90. TM & © Warner Bros. Inc.

Lunch box, plastic. Thermos Company, 1977. Bugs Bunny, Porky Pig, and Daffy Duck are shown on a stage. 7.5" tall. $20-35. TM & © Warner Bros. Inc.

Lunch box, plastic. Thermos Company, 1997. Bugs Bunny and friends are pictured against a festive background. 7.5" tall. $15-20. TM & © Warner Bros. Inc.

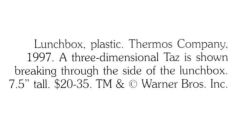

Lunchbox, plastic. Thermos Company, 1997. A three-dimensional Taz is shown breaking through the side of the lunchbox. 7.5" tall. $20-35. TM & © Warner Bros. Inc.

Cookie cutters, plastic. Manufacturer unknown, 1978. Elmer Fudd and Tweety. Approximately 5" tall. $15-20 each. TM & © Warner Bros. Inc.

Waffle iron, metal/plastic. Toastmaster, 1991. This waffle iron makes breakfast in the shape of Bug Bunny's head. 10.5" tall. $45-60. TM & © Warner Bros. Inc.

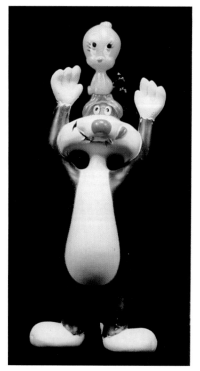

Cake decoration, plastic. Wilton Enterprises, 1978. Tweety is perched on Sylvester's head. 6" tall. $15-20. TM & © Warner Bros. Inc.

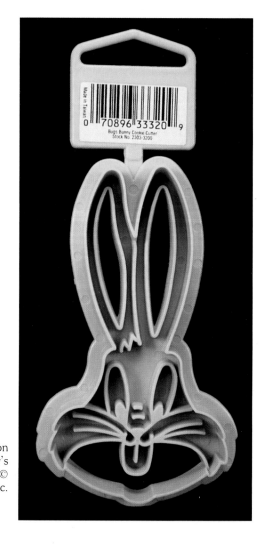

Cookie cutter, plastic. Wilton Enterprises, 1997. Bugs Bunny's head. 5.5" tall. $5-10. TM & © Warner Bros. Inc.

Cake decorations, plastic. Wilton Enterprises, 1978. Bugs Bunny is shown laying down in a garden of carrots. 3.5" tall. $20-35 set. TM & © Warner Bros. Inc.

Cake decorations, plastic. Wilton Enterprises, 1978. Petunia and Sylvester candle holders. 3" tall. $5-10 each. TM & © Warner Bros. Inc.

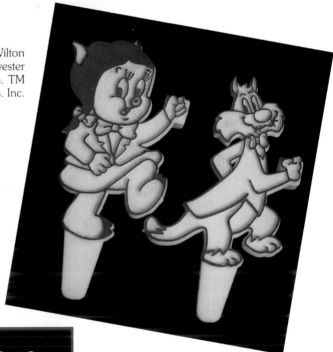

Cake decorations, ceramic. Manufacturer unknown, 1998. Sylvester, Tweety, and Bugs Bunny. Under 3" tall. $10-15 each. TM & © Warner Bros. Inc.

Cake decorations, ceramic. Manufacturer unknown, 1998. Daffy Duck, Taz, and Marvin the Martian. Under 3" tall. $10-15 each. TM & © Warner Bros. Inc.

Cake decorations/candles. Wilton Enterprises, 1994. Bugs Bunny and friends candles. Approximately 2.5" tall. $5-10 set. TM & © Warner Bros. Inc.

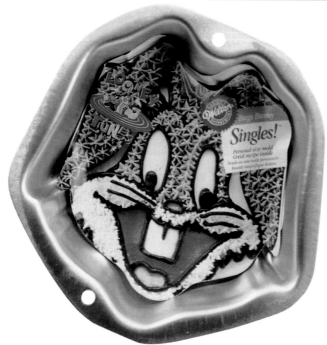

Cake mold, metal. Wilton Enterprises, 1996. Singles personal size mold. Bugs Bunny. 5" tall. $5-10. TM & © Warner Bros. Inc.

Pez dispenser, plastic. Pez Candy, Inc., 1995. Taz, Speedy Gonzales, Yosemite Sam, Tweety, and Sylvester. All are under 5" tall. $5-10 each. TM & © Warner Bros. Inc.

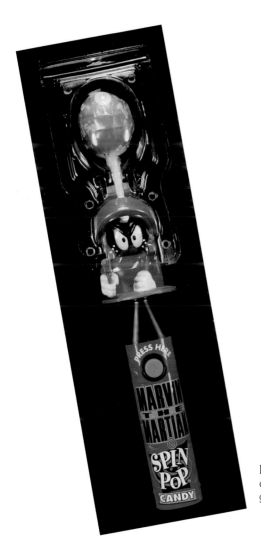

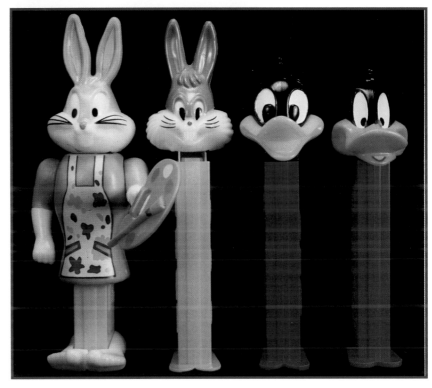

Pez dispenser, plastic. Pez Candy, Inc. Two different versions of Bugs Bunny and Daffy Duck. Bugs Bunny (1993) is shown with an artist outfit from the "body parts" series. All clothing and accessories are removable. $15-20. Bugs Bunny with solid gray ears and tear shaped eyes (1978). $10-15. Daffy Duck (1978) with a yellow beak and rounded eyes. $10-15. Daffy Duck (1993) with an orange beak and oval eyes. $5-10. All are under 5" tall. TM & © Warner Bros. Inc.

Lollipop holder, plastic. Cap Toys, Inc., 1995. Spin Pop candy. When the button is pushed, Marvin the Martian's gun moves. 9" tall. $5-10. TM & © Warner Bros. Inc.

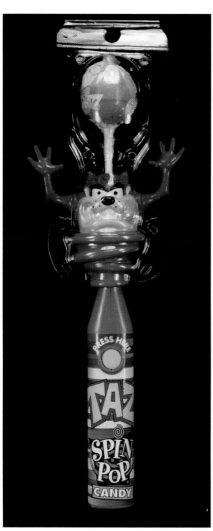

Candy container, tin. Jacobs Suchard, Inc., 1989. Brach's promotion commemorating Bugs Bunny's 50th birthday. Container originally had jelly beans in it. Caption: "Happy birthday Bugs." 6.25" tall. $10-15. TM & © Warner Bros. Inc.

Lollipop holder, plastic. Cap Toys, Inc., 1995. Spin Pop candy. When the button is pushed, Taz spins. 9" tall. $5-10. TM & © Warner Bros. Inc.

Lollipop holder, plastic. Cap Toys, Inc., 1998. Spin Pop candy. When the button is pushed, Sylvester reaches for Tweety. 9" tall. $5-10. TM & © Warner Bros. Inc.

Candy container, tin. Jacobs Suchard, Inc., 1990. Brach's promotion commemorating Bugs Bunny's 50th birthday. Container originally had candy corn in it. Caption: "Looney Tunes school bus." 6.25" tall. $10-15. TM & © Warner Bros. Inc.

Candy container, plastic. Russell Stover Candies, 1997. Bugs Bunny is shown on top of a casket. When the container is opened, music plays. Caption: "Bugs mummy." 6.25" tall. $15-20. TM & © Warner Bros. Inc.

Candy container, cardboard. Russell Stover Candies, 1997. Bugs Bunny is shown dressed as a mummy. 6.25" tall. $5-10. TM & © Warner Bros. Inc.

Candy container, cardboard. Russell Stover Candies, 1997. Daffy Duck is shown as "Duck-Enstein." 6.25" tall. $5-10. TM & © Warner Bros. Inc.

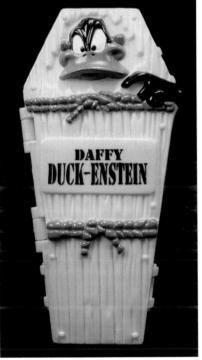

Candy container, plastic. Russell Stover Candies, 1997. Daffy Duck is shown on top of a casket. When the container is opened, music plays. Caption: "Daffy Duck-Enstein." 6.25" tall. $15-20. TM & © Warner Bros. Inc.

Candy container, tin. Russell Stover Candies, 1997. The tin contained one carmel bar, one Looney Tunes figurine, and a sticker. Marvin the Martian and Wile E. Coyote surprise tins. 4" tall. $10-15 each. TM & © Warner Bros. Inc.

Candy container, tin. Russell Stover Candies, 1997. The tin contained one carmel bar, one Looney Tunes figurine, and a sticker. Taz and Bugs Bunny surprise tins. 4" tall. $10-15 each. TM & © Warner Bros. Inc.

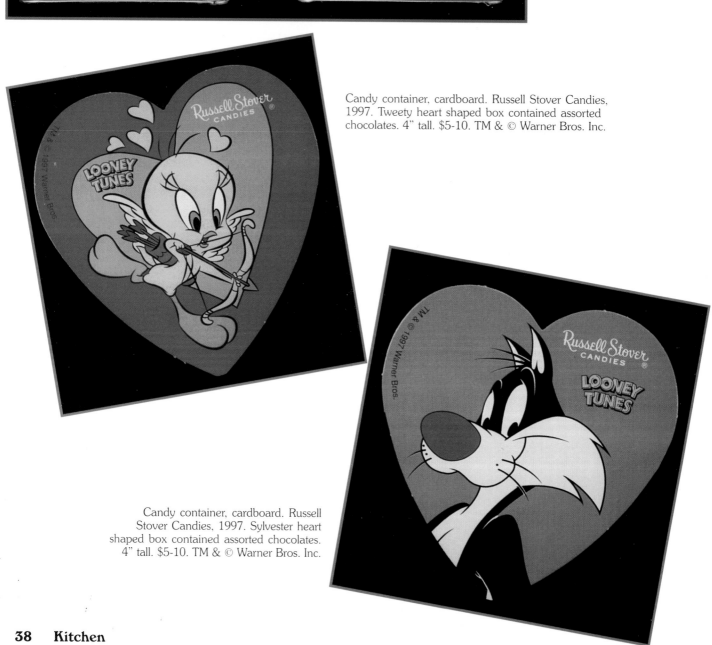

Candy container, cardboard. Russell Stover Candies, 1997. Tweety heart shaped box contained assorted chocolates. 4" tall. $5-10. TM & © Warner Bros. Inc.

Candy container, cardboard. Russell Stover Candies, 1997. Sylvester heart shaped box contained assorted chocolates. 4" tall. $5-10. TM & © Warner Bros. Inc.

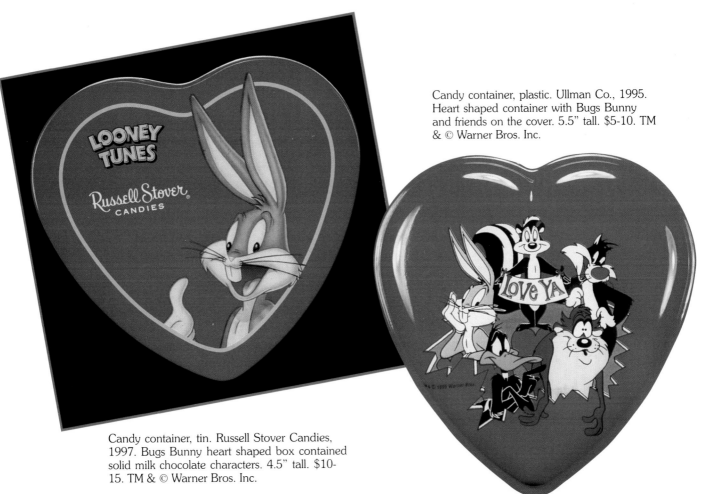

Candy container, plastic. Ullman Co., 1995.
Heart shaped container with Bugs Bunny
and friends on the cover. 5.5" tall. $5-10. TM
& © Warner Bros. Inc.

Candy container, tin. Russell Stover Candies,
1997. Bugs Bunny heart shaped box contained
solid milk chocolate characters. 4.5" tall. $10-
15. TM & © Warner Bros. Inc.

Box. Bayer Corporation, 1996. "Bugs Bunny complete vitamins."
4.5" tall. $5-10. TM & © Warner Bros. Inc.

Box. Kraft Foods, Inc., 1994. "Macaroni & Cheese"
dinner. The pasta is in the shape of Bugs Bunny and
friends. 7" tall. $15-20. TM & © Warner Bros. Inc.

Box. Kraft Foods, Inc., 1997. "Handi-snacks. Cheez'n crackers." A free punch out postcard was included on the back of the package. Complete set of five. 5" tall. $20-35. TM & © Warner Bros. Inc.

Box. Betty Crocker/General Mills, Inc., 1995. "Bugs Bunny and friends snacks made with fruit." 5.75" tall. $15-20. TM & © Warner Bros. Inc.

Box. Post/Kraft Foods, Inc., 1997. "Waffle Crisp" cereal. A free cartoon kit of either Taz or Daffy Duck was included. 11.75" tall. $15-20. TM & © Warner Bros. Inc.

Box. Post/Kraft Foods, Inc., 1997. "Frosted Shredded Wheat" cereal. A free cartoon kit of either Sylvester or Marvin the Martian was included. 11.75" tall. $15-20. TM & © Warner Bros. Inc.

Mugs, Glasses & Cups

Mug, ceramic. Applause, Inc., 1991. The mug is in the shape of Road Runner's head. 3.5" tall. $15-20. TM & © Warner Bros. Inc.

Mug, ceramic. Matrix Industries, Ltd., 1997. Sylvester is shown with snowflakes in the background. 4" tall. $5-10. TM & © Warner Bros. Inc.

Mug, ceramic. Applause, Inc., 1994. Sylvester is shown against a purple background. 4" tall. $5-10. TM & © Warner Bros. Inc.

Translite advertisement. McDonald's promotion, 1995. A Looney Tunes "plays to go" cup was given away with an "Extra Value Meal." The translite would have been displayed as part of the menu. 13.75" tall. $10-15. TM & © Warner Bros. Inc.

Mug, plastic. Whirley. Wal-Mart Collector series/Coca-Cola promotion, 1994. Road Runner. 5.75" tall. $10-15. TM & © Warner Bros. Inc.

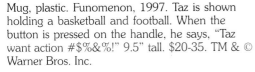

Glass. Welch's collector series promotion, 1994. Each glass originally came with jelly inside. Bugs Bunny (#1 in series). Complete set of 12. 4" tall. $5-10. TM & © Warner Bros. Inc.

Mug, plastic. Funomenon, 1997. Taz is shown holding a basketball and football. When the button is pressed on the handle, he says, "Taz want action #$%&%!" 9.5" tall. $20-35. TM & © Warner Bros. Inc.

Glass. Pepsi collector series promotion, 1973. Porky Pig. 6.25" tall. $10-15. TM & © Warner Bros. Inc.

Mugs, Glasses & Cups   43

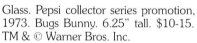

Big sipper, plastic. Monogram Products, Inc., 1996. Sylvester is holding Tweety in one hand. 10" tall. $5-10. TM & © Warner Bros. Inc.

Glass. Pepsi collector series promotion, 1976. Pepé Le Pew is shown holding a garden hose that Daffy Duck has tied in a knot. 6.25" tall. $25-40. TM & © Warner Bros. Inc.

Big sipper, plastic. Monogram Products, Inc., 1996. Taz is shown in a tornado. 7.5" tall. $5-10. TM & © Warner Bros. Inc.

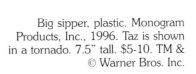

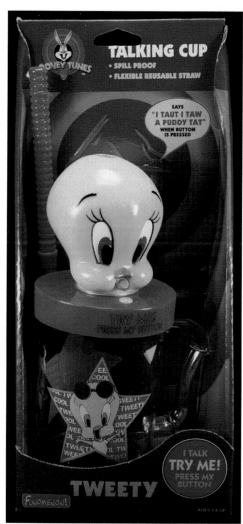

Above: Big sipper, plastic. Monogram Products, Inc., 1996. Marvin the Martian. 10" tall. $5-10. TM & © Warner Bros. Inc.

Top center: Cup, plastic. Funomenon, 1997. Bugs Bunny talking spill proof cup. When the button is pressed, Bugs Bunny says, "Eh, What's up, Doc?" 9" tall. $10-15. TM & © Warner Bros. Inc.

Top right: Cup, plastic. Funomenon, 1997. Tweety talking spill proof cup. When the button is pressed, Tweety says, "I taut I taw a puddy tat." 9" tall. $10-15. TM & © Warner Bros. Inc.

Bottom left: Cup, plastic. Funomenon, 1997. Taz talking spill proof cup. When the button is pressed, Taz says, "Taz love drink $?&*!" 9" tall. $10-15. TM & © Warner Bros. Inc.

Bottom right: Juice bottle, plastic. Fun Designs, Inc., 1996. Bugs Bunny shaped bottle with belt clip on back. 6.5" tall. $5-10. TM & © Warner Bros. Inc.

Bath

Soap dispenser, ceramic. Certified International Corp., 1993. Bugs Bunny. 6.5" tall. $25-40. TM & © Warner Bros. Inc.

Soap dispenser, ceramic. Certified International Corp., 1993. Sylvester. 5.5" tall. $25-40. TM & © Warner Bros. Inc.

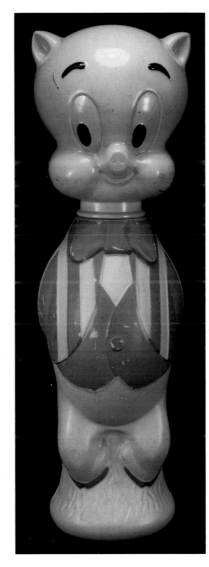

Soakie, plastic. Colgate-Polmolive Company, N/A. Porky Pig is shown wearing a blue tie and striped shirt. The container originally held bubble bath liquid. 9.5" tall. $30-45. TM & © Warner Bros. Inc.

Bubble bath container, plastic. Minnetonka Brands, Inc., 1997. Bugs Bunny is shown leaning against a pink bar of soap. 8.5" tall. $10-15. TM & © Warner Bros. Inc.

Bubble bath container, plastic. Minnetonka Brands, Inc., 1997. Taz is shown submerged in bubbles. 8" tall. $10-15. TM & © Warner Bros. Inc.

Bubble bath container, plastic. Minnetonka Brands, Inc., 1997. Sylvester is holding a blue brush while Tweety rests on his head. 9" tall. $10-15. TM & © Warner Bros. Inc.

Bubble bath container, plastic. Minnetonka Brands, Inc., 1997. Daffy Duck is shown leaning against a blue bar of soap. 7.5" tall. $10-15. TM & © Warner Bros. Inc.

Bubble bath container, plastic. Prelude UK, Ltd., 1995. Tweety is wearing a blue bath robe. 9" tall. $15-20. TM & © Warner Bros. Inc.

Bubble bath container, plastic. Prelude UK, Ltd., 1996. Taz is wearing boxing gloves and a heavy weight belt. 8" tall. $15-20. TM & © Warner Bros. Inc.

Bubble bath container, plastic. Prelude UK, Ltd., 1993. Daffy Duck is wearing a shark costume. 10.5" tall. $20-35. TM & © Warner Bros. Inc.

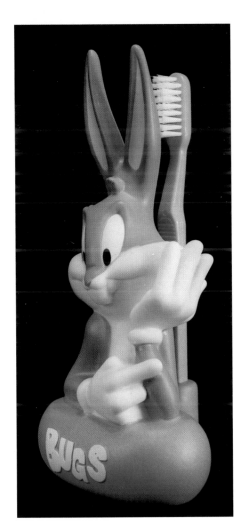

Toothbrush holder, plastic. Minnetonka Brands, Inc., 1996. A toothbrush is concealed behind Bugs Bunny. 7.25" tall. $10-15. TM & © Warner Bros. Inc.

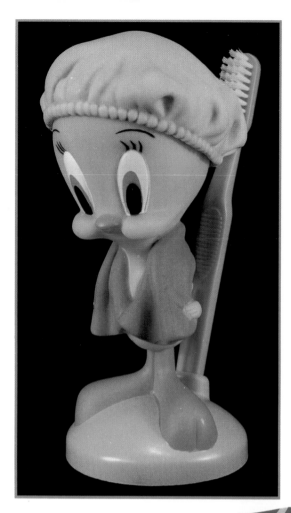

Toothbrush holder, plastic. Minnetonka Brands, Inc., 1996. A toothbrush is concealed behind Tweety. 6" tall. $10-15. TM & © Warner Bros. Inc.

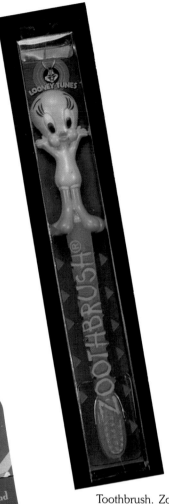

Toothpaste. Zooth, Inc., 1996. "Zoothpaste." Tropical fruit flavored toothpaste topped with Tweety. 7" tall. $5-10. TM & © Warner Bros. Inc.

Toothbrush. Zooth, Inc., 1997. "Zoothbrush." Toothbrush topped with Tweety. 6" tall. $5-10. TM & © Warner Bros. Inc.

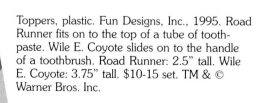

Toppers, plastic. Fun Designs, Inc., 1995. Road Runner fits on to the top of a tube of toothpaste. Wile E. Coyote slides on to the handle of a toothbrush. Road Runner: 2.5" tall. Wile E. Coyote: 3.75" tall. $10-15 set. TM & © Warner Bros. Inc.

Toppers, plastic. Fun Designs, Inc., 1995.
Tweety fits on to the top of a tube of toothpaste.
Sylvester slides on to the handle of a tooth-
brush. Tweety: 1.75" tall. Sylvester: 3.75" tall.
$5-10 set. TM & © Warner Bros. Inc.

Electric toothbrush, plastic. Janex Corporation, 1973.
Bugs Bunny is shown leaning against a carrot shaped
toothbrush holder. Caption: "Eh, Brush up, Doc!"
Battery operated. 8.5" tall. $35-50. TM & © Warner
Bros. Inc.

Electric toothbrush, plastic. Janex Corporation, 1996. Taz is shown on the handle of an
electric toothbrush. Battery operated. 7.5"
tall. $15-20. TM & © Warner Bros. Inc.

Perfume bottle, glass/resin. Manufacturer unknown, 1997. Tweety shaped stopper. Clear glass base. 4.5" tall. $35-50. TM & © Warner Bros. Inc.

Mirror, plastic. DuCair Bioessence/A division of Tsumura International, Inc., 1990. Bugs Bunny is shown on an orange pocket mirror. 4.75" tall. $5-10. TM & © Warner Bros. Inc.

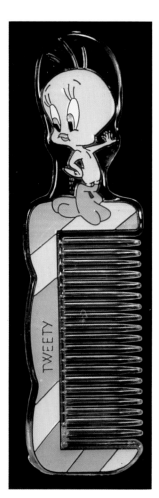

Comb, plastic. World Trend, Inc., 1997. Tweety decorates the comb's handle. 5" tall. $5-10. TM & © Warner Bros. Inc.

Perfume bottle, ceramic/glass. Manufacturer unknown, 1995. Penelope is shown spraying some perfume on Pepé Le Pew. 5" tall. $40-55. TM & © Warner Bros. Inc.

Adhesive bandages. American White Cross, 1995. Two different versions. Bugs Bunny or Wile E. Coyote. One size. $5-10 each. TM & © Warner Bros. Inc.

Perfume bottle, glass/resin. Manufacturer unknown, 1997. Pepé Le Pew is shown sitting on top of a heart shaped bottle. 6.5" tall. $40-55. TM & © Warner Bros. Inc.

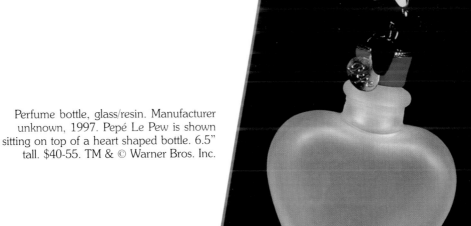

General Household

Lawn sprinkler, resin. Manufacturer unknown, 1998. Tweety is shown holding a garden hose. 6" tall. $35-50. TM & © Warner Bros. Inc.

Planter, plastic. Hei, 1994. Caption: "Fun on the farm." Seeds were originally included to be planted in the green section of the base. 5" tall. $10-15. TM & © Warner Bros. Inc.

Telephone, plastic. Toshiba of Canada, Ltd., 1996. Bugs Bunny is the hand held receiver. The rock base conceals the push button key pad. 9" tall. $65-80. TM & © Warner Bros. Inc.

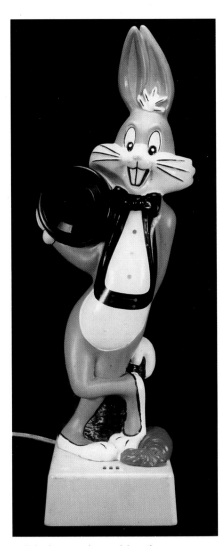

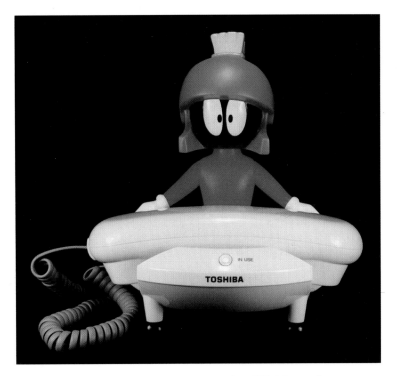

Telephone, plastic. Toshiba of Canada, Ltd., 1997. Marvin the Martian is shown riding in his space ship. 9" tall. $85-100. TM & © Warner Bros. Inc.

Telephone, plastic. Manufacturer unknown, 1982. Bugs Bunny is the hand held receiver. The push button key pad is concealed underneath the base. 11.5" tall. $65-80. TM & © Warner Bros. Inc.

Frame, resin. Decorel, Inc., 1994. Wile E. Coyote is shown riding a rocket ship. 6.75" tall. $20-35. TM & © Warner Bros. Inc.

Frame, resin. Manufacturer unknown, 1995. Marvin the Martian and K-9 are shown standing in front of a space ship. 7" tall. $15-20. TM & © Warner Bros. Inc.

Nightlight, plastic. Happiness Express, Inc., 1994. This nightlight is in the shape of a television set. The television glows and projects an image on the ceiling. 8" tall. $20-35. TM & © Warner Bros. Inc.

Frame, plastic. Matrix Industries, Ltd., 1997. Bugs Bunny is shown on the corner of a black frame. 8.75" tall. $15-20. TM & © Warner Bros. Inc.

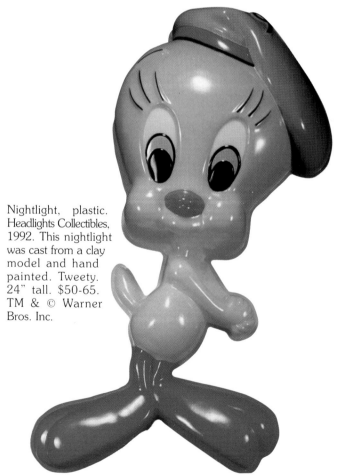

Nightlight, plastic. Headlights Collectibles, 1992. This nightlight was cast from a clay model and hand painted. Tweety. 24" tall. $50-65. TM & © Warner Bros. Inc.

Nodder statue, resin. Manufacturer unknown, 1998. With the help of a magnet, Pepé Le Pew tries to kiss Penelope. She has a clothespin on her nose. Caption: "Ze attraction is magnetic, No?" 5" tall. $125-140. TM & © Warner Bros. Inc.

Lamp with nodder statue, resin/metal. Casal/Underwriters Laboratories, Inc., 1996. Bugs Bunny is shown standing on top of four reels of film. 15.5" tall. $95-110. TM & © Warner Bros. Inc.

Nodder statue, resin. Manufacturer unknown, 1993. "Classic Looney Tunes Bobbing Head" series. Pepé Le Pew. 8" tall. $65-80. TM & © Warner Bros. Inc.

Nodder statue, resin. Manufacturer unknown, 1993. "Classic Looney Tunes Bobbing Head" series. Tweety. 8" tall. $60-75. TM & © Warner Bros. Inc.

Nodder statue, resin. Manufacturer unknown, 1996. Road Runner is shown eating free bird seed. Wile E. Coyote is shown with an anvil on his head. 9.5" tall. $125-140. TM & © Warner Bros. Inc.

Statue, bisque. Manufacturer unknown, 1975. Porky Pig. 2.5" tall. $45-60. TM & © Warner Bros. Inc.

Statue, resin. Manufacturer unknown, 1996. Sylvester and Jr. are shown fishing. 8" tall. $35-50. TM & © Warner Bros. Inc.

Author's note: *I keep this statue on the top shelf in my refrigerator. It's fun to see people smile when they open the door!*

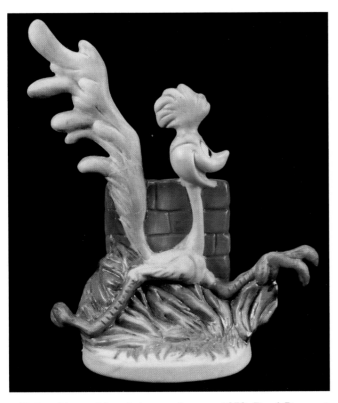

Statue, bisque. Manufacturer unknown, 1979. Road Runner is shown running next to a brick wall. 5.25" tall. $65-80. TM & © Warner Bros. Inc.

Statue, bisque. Manufacturer unknown, 1979. Sylvester is shown sitting on a tree stump. 5" tall. $60-75. TM & © Warner Bros. Inc.

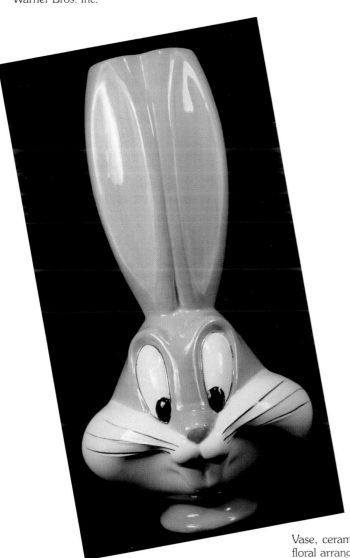

Screen saver/mouse pad set. Berkeley Systems, Inc., 1994. The enclosed disk can be downloaded to put a Taz screen saver on to a computer monitor. One size. $15-20. TM & © Warner Bros. Inc.

Vase, ceramic. Manufacturer unknown, 1997. Bugs Bunny's ears hold small floral arrangements. 10" tall. $30-45. TM & © Warner Bros. Inc.

Remote control holder, fabric. Blue Ridge: The Item Co., 1995. Sylvester is weighted to balance over the arm of a sofa or chair. 16" tall. $20-35. TM & © Warner Bros. Inc.

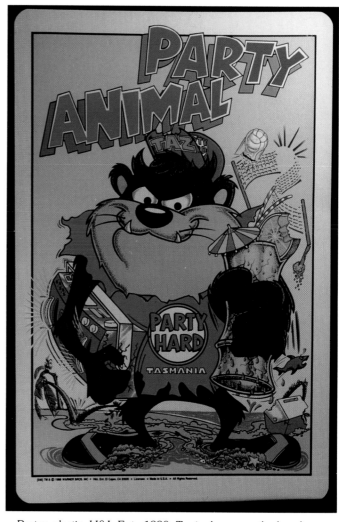

Poster, plastic. H&L Ent., 1990. Taz is shown on the beach. Caption: "Party animal. Party hard Tasmania." 17" tall. $10-15. TM & © Warner Bros. Inc.

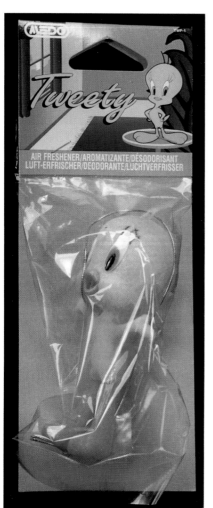

Air Freshner. Medo Industries, Inc., 1996. Tweety. 4" tall. $5-10. TM & © Warner Bros. Inc.

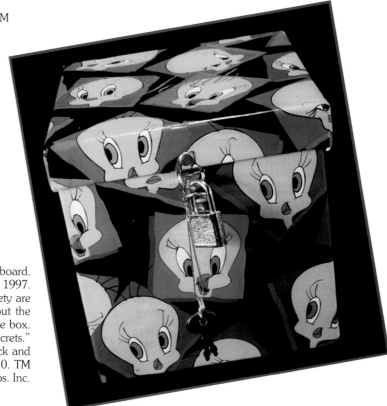

Secrets box, cardboard. Once Upon a Rose, 1997. Pictures of Tweety are shown throughout the pattern on the box. Caption: "Secrets." Complete with lock and key. 5.25" tall. $5-10. TM & © Warner Bros. Inc.

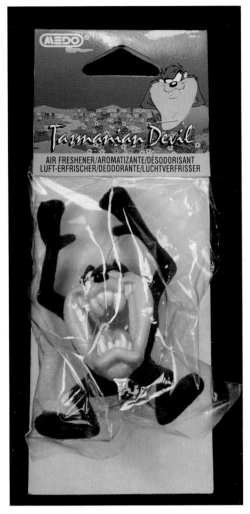

Backpack, nylon/polyester. Manufacturer unknown, 1994. Bugs Bunny's head. 12" tall. $10-15. TM & © Warner Bros. Inc.

Air Freshner. Medo Industries, Inc., 1996. Yosemite Sam. Caption: "Back off you varmint!" 4" tall. $5-10. TM & © Warner Bros. Inc.

Air Freshner. Medo Industries, Inc., 1996. Taz. 3.75" tall. $5-10. TM & © Warner Bros. Inc.

Backpack, fabric/ suede. Holiday Fair, Inc./Mischief Makers, 1996. A dark green backpack is accented with embroidered Looney Tunes characters. One size. $20-35. TM & © Warner Bros. Inc.

Key ring, pewter. Rawcliffe, 1995. Road Runner. 4.25" tall. $10-15. TM & © Warner Bros. Inc.

Iron on T-shirt decal. Roach, 1978. Tweety. 9.5" tall. $10-15. TM & © Warner Bros. Inc.

Opposite page:
Top left: Pattern. Butterick Pattern Service, 1978. Patterns and directions to make a Tweety costume are included. One size. $15-20. TM & © Warner Bros. Inc.

Top right: Pattern. Butterick Pattern Service, 1990. Patterns and directions to make either a Sylvester or Tweety costume are included. One size. $15-20. TM & © Warner Bros. Inc.

Bottom left: Pattern. McCall Pattern Company, 1986. Patterns and directions to make either a Sylvester or Tweety costume are included. One size. $15-20. TM & © Warner Bros. Inc.

Bottom right: Halloween costume, plastic/fabric. Collegeville Flag & Manufacturing, Co., 1987. Bugs Bunny. Children's sizes. $25-40. TM & © Warner Bros. Inc.

Buttons, plastic. Manufacturer unknown, 1989. Yosemite Sam, Porky Pig, Elmer Fudd, and Sylvester. 0.5" in diameter. $5-10 each. *Courtesy of Tracey Curry.* TM & © Warner Bros. Inc.

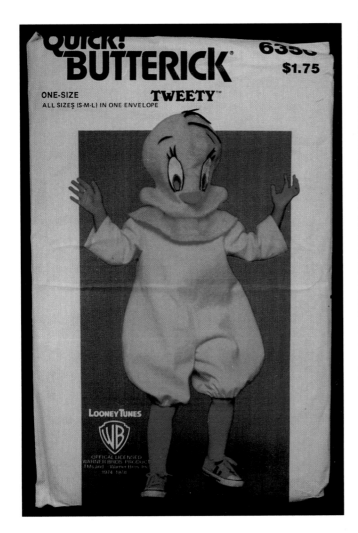

Collector Plates

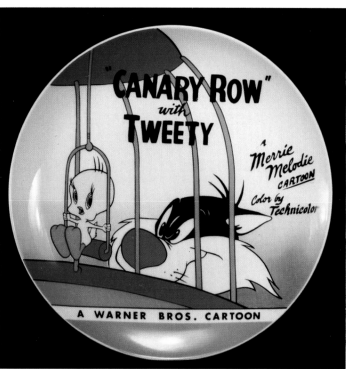

Collector plate, ceramic. Manufacturer unknown, 1994. Titled "Pepé Le Pew in *Who Scent You?* (1960)." For decorative use only. 9" in diameter. $25-40. TM & © Warner Bros. Inc.

Collector plate, ceramic. Manufacturer unknown, 1994. Titled "*Canary Row* with Tweety (1950)." For decorative use only. 9" in diameter. $20-35. TM & © Warner Bros. Inc.

Collector plate, ceramic. Manufacturer unknown, 1995. Limited edition of 2,500 pieces. This was the third plate in the series. Sketches of Pepé Le Pew and Penelope are shown. For decorative use only. 10.25" in diameter. $45-60. TM & © Warner Bros. Inc.

Collector plate, ceramic. Manufacturer unknown, 1993. Bugs Bunny and friends are shown dressed in Medieval attire. Titled *"King Arthurs' Court • 1978."* For decorative use only. 6.5" in diameter. $35-50. TM & © Warner Bros. Inc.

Collector plate, ceramic. Manufacturer unknown, 1993. Elmer Fudd and Daffy Duck. Titled *"Rabbit Seasoning • 1952."* For decorative use only. 6.5" in diameter. $35-50. TM & © Warner Bros. Inc.

Collector plate, ceramic. Manufacturer unknown, 1993. Bugs Bunny is shown dressed as a Matador. Titled *"Bully for Bugs • 1953."* For decorative use only. 6.5" in diameter. $35-50. TM & © Warner Bros. Inc.

Collector plate, ceramic. Manufacturer unknown, 1993. Wile E. Coyote is shown chasing after Road Runner. Titled *"Fast and Furry-ous • 1949."* For decorative use only. 6.5" in diameter. $40-55. TM & © Warner Bros. Inc.

Clocks

Alarm clock, plastic. Janex Corporation, 1978. Talking clock with revolving action. Sylvester chases Tweety. 8" tall. $110-125. TM & © Warner Bros. Inc.

Alarm clock, plastic. Westclox, 1997. Talking clock with digital display. Bugs Bunny is shown sleeping in his bed. Taz is shown peeking into the rabbit hole. When the demo button is pressed, Taz says, "Wake up." Bugs Bunny replies, "Okay, Okay, Doc. Keep your shirt on." 6.25" tall. $50-65. TM & © Warner Bros. Inc.

Alarm clock, plastic. Westclox, 1996. Digital display. Tweety is shown tucked into his nest. The snooze alarm is turned off by pressing Tweety's head. 5.5" tall. $30-45. TM & © Warner Bros. Inc.

Alarm clock, plastic. Westclox, 1995. Digital display. Taz is shown popping out of a rock. 5.5" tall. $30-45. TM & © Warner Bros. Inc.

Alarm clock, plastic. Westclox, 1994. Wile E. Coyote is riding on a powered skateboard. 3.75" tall. $25-40. TM & © Warner Bros. Inc.

Alarm clock, plastic. Westclox,1997. A 3-D Taz is shown eating an alarm clock. 5" tall. $30-45. TM & © Warner Bros. Inc.

Alarm clock, plastic. Westclox, 1994. Taz is shown against a blue, green, and yellow background. 4.25" tall. $20-35. TM & © Warner Bros. Inc.

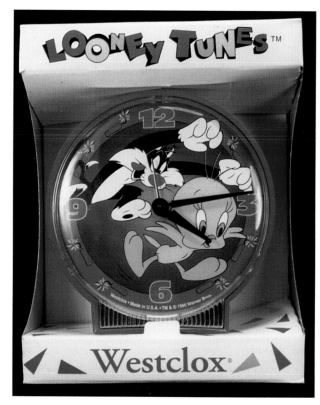

Alarm clock, plastic. Westclox, 1995. Sylvester is shown chasing after Tweety. 4.5" tall. $20-35. TM & © Warner Bros. Inc.

Alarm clock, metal/plastic. Westclox, 1995. Taz is shown against a red background. 5.5" tall. $30-45. TM & © Warner Bros. Inc.

Clock, resin. Manufacturer unknown, 1994. Taz is shown at the office. 5.25" tall. $30-45. TM & © Warner Bros. Inc.

Clock, resin. Westclox Canada/General Time Corp., 1997. Hand painted. Taz is shown lifting weights. 3" tall. $20-35. TM & © Warner Bros. Inc.

Clock, resin. Westclox Canada/General Time Corp., 1997. Hand painted. Tweety and Sylvester are shown holding some balloons. 3" tall. $20-35. TM & © Warner Bros. Inc.

Clock, plastic/cardboard. Can You Imagine Corp., 1994. A pendulum in the shape of Taz swings back and forth. 10.25" tall. $30-45. TM & © Warner Bros. Inc.

Clocks   69

Banks

Bank, vinyl. Home Craft Prod., 1972. Bugs Bunny is shown in a barrel of carrots. Caption: "What's up, Doc?" 12.5" tall. $30-45. TM & © Warner Bros. Inc.

Bank, plastic/rubber. R. Dakin & Co., 1971. Road Runner is standing on a sand dune. 11" tall. $65-80. TM & © Warner Bros. Inc.

Bank, tin. Giftco, Inc., 1996. The top cover of the bank shows Wile E. Coyote riding on an "ACME" rocket. Caption: "Bombs away!" 4" tall. $20-35. TM & © Warner Bros. Inc.

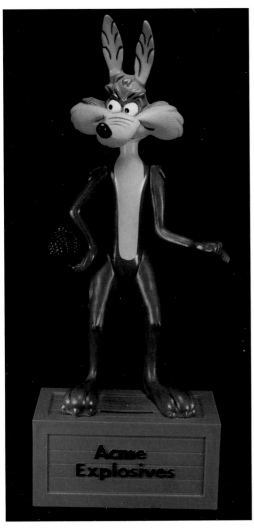

Bank, plastic. Applause, Inc., 1997. Tweety is holding an oversized mallet. 8" tall. $15-20. TM & © Warner Bros. Inc.

Bank, plastic/rubber. R. Dakin & Co., 1971. Wile E. Coyote is standing on a box labeled "ACME explosives." 12" tall. $60-75. TM & © Warner Bros. Inc.

Bank, plastic. Manufacturer unknown, 1996. Marvin the Martian stands next to a space ship. 6.5" tall. $15-20. TM & © Warner Bros. Inc.

Bank, plastic. Applause, Inc., 1997. Taz's smile reveals that he has eaten an "ACME" safe. 8.5" tall. $15-20. TM & © Warner Bros. Inc.

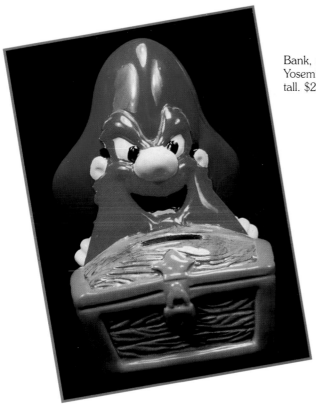

Bank, ceramic. Applause, Inc., 1988.
Yosemite Sam guards a treasure chest. 5.5"
tall. $20-35. TM & © Warner Bros. Inc.

Bank, plastic. Russell Stover Candies,
1997. Bugs Bunny and friends explore a
haunted house. This originally came with
individually foil-wrapped milk chocolate
characters. 6" tall. $15-20. TM & ©
Warner Bros. Inc.

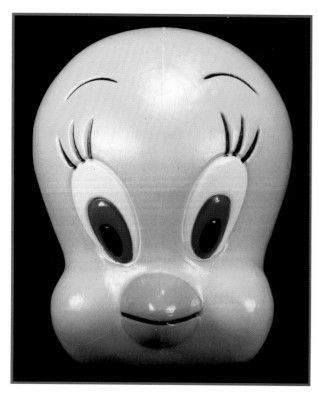

Bank, plastic. Creative Confection Con-
cepts. L.L.C., 1997. This originally came
with multi-colored gumballs. Tweety. 5" tall.
$15-20. TM & © Warner Bros. Inc.

Trinket Boxes

Trinket box, resin. Figi Graphics, 1994. Bugs Bunny is shown in a rose garden. 3.75" tall. $30-45. TM & © Warner Bros. Inc.

Trinket box, ceramic. Manufacturer unknown, 1997. The top portion of Pepé Le Pew's head lifts off the base. 4.5" tall. $35-50. TM & © Warner Bros. Inc.

Trinket box, porcelain. Manufacturer unknown, 1997. Limited edition of 500 pieces. Penelope sits on a pink pillow. When the box is opened, a miniature perfume bottle is revealed. 2.25" tall. $150-165. TM & © Warner Bros. Inc.

Trinket box, porcelain. Manufacturer unknown, 1997. Limited edition of 500 pieces. Sylvester is shown sitting on top of Tweety's bird house. When the box is opened, miniature furniture is shown. 3.25" tall. $145-160. TM & © Warner Bros. Inc.

Trinket box, porcelain. Manufacturer unknown, 1995. Limited edition of 500 pieces. Penelope is shown taking a bubble bath. When the box is opened, a picture of Pepé Le Pew wearing scuba gear is revealed. 2.75" tall. $150-165. TM & © Warner Bros. Inc.

Trinket box, porcelain. Manufacturer unknown, 1997. Limited edition of 500 pieces. Marvin The Martian is shown in a blue space ship. When the box is opened, a picture of Marvin is shown. 3.25" tall. $145-160. TM & © Warner Bros. Inc.

Trinket box, porcelain. Midwest of Cannon Falls, 1996. Bugs Bunny is standing on top of a film reel. 4" tall. $30-45. TM & © Warner Bros. Inc.

Trinket box, porcelain. Midwest of Cannon Falls, 1996. Sylvester is standing on top of a film reel. 3.5" tall. $30-45. TM & © Warner Bros. Inc.

Trinket box, porcelain. Midwest of Cannon Falls, 1996. Taz is standing on top of a film reel. 2.75" tall. $30-45. TM & © Warner Bros. Inc.

Trinket box, porcelain. Midwest of Cannon Falls, 1996. Sylvester is holding Tweety's bird cage. 4.5" tall. $110-125. TM & © Warner Bros. Inc.

Trinket box, porcelain. Midwest of Cannon Falls, 1996. Wile E. Coyote is shown riding a rocket while Road Runner watches. 4" tall. $115-130. TM & © Warner Bros. Inc.

Trinket box, porcelain. Midwest of Cannon Falls, 1996. Bugs Bunny peeks over Elmer Fudd's shoulder while he is hunting. 4.5" tall. $110-125. TM & © Warner Bros. Inc.

Trinket box, porcelain. Manufacturer unknown, 1998. Pepé Le Pew and Penelope are shown in a rowboat. Caption: "Ooh la la." 3" tall. $115-130. TM & © Warner Bros. Inc.

Music Boxes

Snow globe, resin/glass. Matrix Industries, Ltd., 1997. Musical waterball. Wile E. Coyote is shown holding sticks of dynamite. 6" tall. $50-65. TM & © Warner Bros. Inc.

Snow globe, resin/glass. Matrix Industries, Ltd., 1997. Musical waterball. Sylvester is shown sneaking up behind Tweety. 6" tall. $50-65. TM & © Warner Bros. Inc.

Jewelry box, cardboard/plastic. Tri-Star Merchandise, Inc., 1997. Tweety dances to music when the box is opened. 6.5" tall. $15-20. TM & © Warner Bros. Inc.

Jewelry & Coins

Pin, metal/rhinestones. Manufacturer unknown, N/A. Tweety. 1.75" tall. $20-35. TM & © Warner Bros. Inc.

Coin, 0.999 pure silver/one troy ounce. Rarities Mint, Inc., 1990. Rare limited proof edition. Project director: Peter Bloodsworth. Sculptor: Don Winton. Elmer Fudd is shown in his hunting attire. Caption: "Cwazy wabbit!" Reverse side shows Bugs Bunny's 50th birthday logo. This coin is the second in a series of twelve. 1.5" in diameter. $35-50. TM & © Warner Bros. Inc.

Pin, metal/enamel. Starline Creations, Inc., 1997. This pin was issued to commemorate the "Official Looney Tunes Stamp Collection." Caption: "What's up, Doc?" 1.75" tall. $10-15. TM & © Warner Bros. Inc.

Pin, metal. Button Exchange, Ltd., 1992. Wile E. Coyote. Caption: "Elect a Real Super Genius. Wile E. Coyote for President." 1.75" in diameter. $5-10. TM & © Warner Bros. Inc.

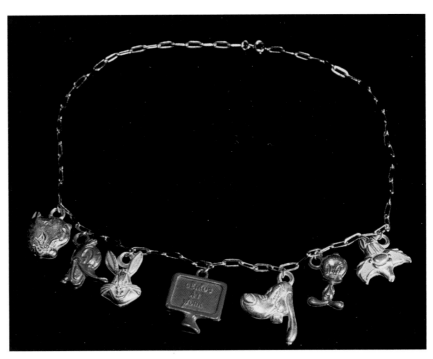

Charms, plastic. Manufacturer unknown, N/A. Porky Pig, Daffy Duck, Bugs Bunny, "Genius at work" sign, K-9, Tweety, and Sylvester. The chain pictured is not original. Each charm is approximately 0.5" tall. $15-20 each. TM & © Warner Bros. Inc.

Watch. Armitron, 1994. Daffy Duck is shown looking at a backwards watch dial. Tin case. One size. $30-45. TM & © Warner Bros. Inc.

Pin, metal. Button Exchange, Ltd., 1992. Road Runner. Caption: "Accelerati Incredibulus." 1.75" in diameter. $10-15. TM & © Warner Bros. Inc.

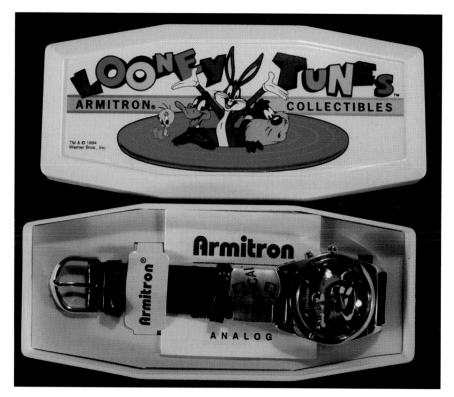

Watch. Armitron, 1994. Pepé Le Pew is shown with Penelope on a purple and pink background. Musical. Plastic case. One size. $50-65. TM & © Warner Bros. Inc.

Watch. Armitron, 1993. Taz is shown kicking a soccer ball. Water resistant. One size. $30-45. TM & © Warner Bros. Inc.

Watch. Armitron, 1994. Marvin the Martian is shown against a black and blue background. Plastic case. One size. $45-60. TM & © Warner Bros. Inc.

Watch. Armitron, 1997. Tweety is shown against a pink background. Plastic case. One size. $20-35. TM & © Warner Bros. Inc.

Watch. Laserchron Watches, 1990. Official licensee Major League Baseball. 3-D Holographic. Foghorn Leghorn New York Mets watch. 26 different teams were produced. One size. $25-40. TM & © Warner Bros. Inc.

Watch. Good Stuff, 1993. When the watch is moved, Taz shows either the time or curse symbols. One size. $20-35. TM & © Warner Bros. Inc.

Watch. Laserchron Watches, 1990. Official licensee Major League Baseball. 3-D Holographic. Tweety St. Louis Cardinals watch. 26 different teams were produced. One size. $25-40. TM & © Warner Bros. Inc.

Toys

Pinball game, plastic. Tyco Playtime, Inc., 1993. Taz pinball has fippers, scoring, lights, and sounds. Taz is shown in a desert. Battery operated. 10.5" tall. $60-75. TM & © Warner Bros. Inc.

Promotional flyer. Bally/Midway, 1990. A full size arcade pinball game was produced to celebrate Bugs Bunny's birthday ball. Coin operated. One size. $10-15. TM & © Warner Bros. Inc.

Game, plastic/cardboard. Manufacturer unknown, 1982. Wile E. Coyote is shown on a pogo stick. Road Runner is shown on a scooter. 2.5" tall. $10-15. TM & © Warner Bros. Inc.

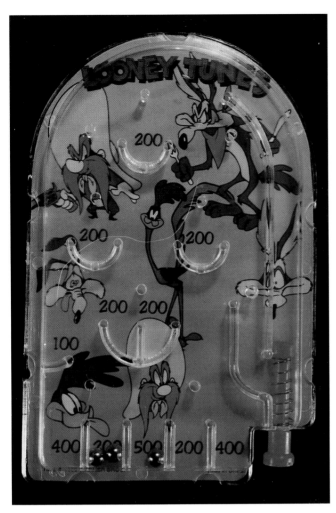

Animation toy, cardboard. Manufacturer unknown, 1957. "Looney Toonavision." When the knobs are turned, parts of each character's face intermix. 12.75" tall. $50-65. TM & © Warner Bros. Inc.

Pinball game, plastic. Ace Novelty Co., Inc., 1995. Hand held mini pinball game with Looney Tunes characters. 4.5" tall. $5-10. TM & © Warner Bros. Inc.

Cartoon maker, cardboard/metal. Metal Moss Manufacturing Co., N/A. "Cartoon-O-Graph" sketch board. There is a metal pen holder attached to the sketchboard which can be used to trace Looney Tunes/Merrie Melodies characters. 14.5" tall. $60-75. TM & © Warner Bros. Inc.

Board game. Whitman/Western Publishing Company, Inc., 1969. "The Road Runner game." The object of the game is for Road Runner to out race Wile E. Coyote. Game includes: one deck of cards, eight Road Runner cut outs, and one Wile E. Coyote cut out. One size. $30-45. TM & © Warner Bros. Inc.

Board game. Whitman/Western Publishing Company, Inc., 1982. "The Road Runner Pop-up game." The object of the game is to successfully get all three of the Road Runner game pieces to the designated cave. Game includes: one gameboard, twelve playing pieces, and one spinner. One size. $60-75. TM & © Warner Bros. Inc.

Board game. Patomike, Inc., 1989. "What's up, Doc? The Bugs Bunny game." This game commemorates Bugs Bunny's 50th birthday. The object of the game is to be the first player to gather Bugs Bunny's presents and bring them to the party. Game includes: one game board, dice, player pieces, and gift cards. One size. $25-40. TM & © Warner Bros. Inc.

Board game. Tyco Industries, Ltd., 1994. "Looney Tunes Smush 'em game." The object of the game is to be the first player to get to the "that's all folks" space without getting smushed. Game includes: one board game, dough, molds, character faces, 3-D parts sheet, spinner, and "ACME" devices. One size. $25-40. TM & © Warner Bros. Inc.

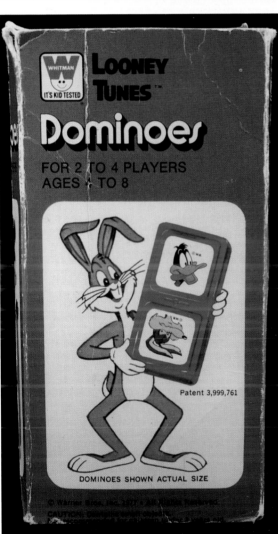

Flash cards. The United States Playing Card Co., 1997. Looney Tunes characters are shown on cards depicting 50 addition problems. 5.5" tall. $5-10. TM & © Warner Bros. Inc.

Dominoes, plastic. Whitman/Western Publishing Company, Inc., 1977. The object of the game is to match the same Looney Tunes characters. 28 pieces. One size. $20-35. TM & © Warner Bros. Inc.

Trivia game. Tyson promotion, 1991. Example of trivia question and answer: "What facial expression is Roadrunner often seen making? Sticking out his tongue." 4" tall. $15-20. TM & © Warner Bros. Inc.

Chatter chum, plastic. Mattel, Inc., 1976. When the cord is pulled from Bugs Bunny's back, he moves his mouth and says, "I like you." 8" tall. $30-45. TM & © Warner Bros. Inc.

Bop bag. Intex Trading, Ltd., 1997. The Taz bop bag is weighted with sand to make it bounce back and forth. One size. $15-20. TM & © Warner Bros. Inc.

Motorcycle toy, vinyl/plastic. Manufacturer unknown, 1995. "Biker Taz." When the red button is pressed under Taz's knee, the motorcycle makes noise and lights flash. 10" tall. $85-100. TM & © Warner Bros. Inc.

Chatter chum, plastic. Mattel, Inc., 1976. When the cord is pulled from Tweety's back, he moves his mouth and says, "Uh oh, Granny a puddy tat." 8" tall. $30-45. TM & © Warner Bros. Inc.

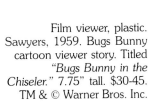

Talking Bugs Bunny, plastic. Tyco Industries, Ltd., 1993. Bugs Bunny says one of three sayings when the buttons are pushed on his back. For example: "What's up, Doc?" "Of course, you know this means war!" and "Whatta maroon! Whatta Ignoramus!" 10.5" tall. $40-55. TM & © Warner Bros. Inc.

Film viewer, plastic. Sawyers, 1959. Bugs Bunny cartoon viewer story. Titled *"Bugs Bunny in the Chiseler."* 7.75" tall. $30-45. TM & © Warner Bros. Inc.

View-Master. GAF Corporation,1959. 21 Stereo pictures. Titled *"Bugs Bunny."* 4.5" tall. $20-35. TM & © Warner Bros. Inc.

Movie. Associated Artists Production Corp. (A.A.P.), N/A. Titled *"Daffy Duck Slept Here."* 8MM Home movie. 3.75" in diameter. $15-20. TM & © Warner Bros. Inc.

Authors note: *In the 1950s, Jack Warner sold a large selection of Warner Bros. films and cartoons to A.A.P. for television distribution. Recently, Warner Bros. reacquired them via Turner Broadcasting Systems, Inc.*

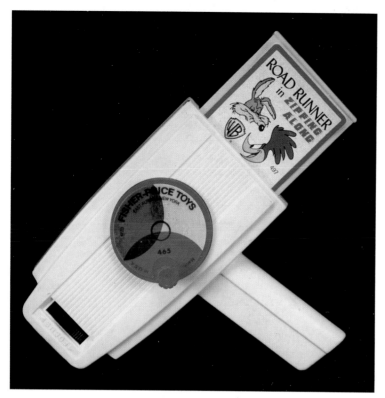

Movie viewer, plastic. Fisher-Price Toys, 1978. When you wind up the knob on the side of the viewer, the film cartridge advances to show a movie. Titled *"Road Runner in Zipping Along."* 6.25" tall. $30-45. TM & © Warner Bros. Inc.

Drawing slate. Landoll, Inc., 1997. Bugs Bunny "crazy slate." 13.5" tall. $5-10. TM & © Warner Bros. Inc.

Marbles, glass. Qualatex, 1988. Wile E. Coyote and Road Runner. 1" in diameter. $15-20 each. TM & © Warner Bros. Inc.

Jacks, plastic. Manufacturer unknown, 1997. Complete with one ball, six solid color jacks, and two multi-colored jacks. One size. $10-15. TM & © Warner Bros. Inc.

Ball, plastic. Spectra Star, 1995. "Collectaballs." The ball is in the shape of Daffy Duck. 3.5" tall. $5-10. TM & © Warner Bros. Inc.

Ball, rubber. Koosh, 1995. Bugs Bunny is shown holding a carrot. 5" tall. $5-10. TM & © Warner Bros. Inc.

Toy, fabric/plastic. Mattel, Inc., 1976. "Bugs Bunny in the music box." When the handle on the side of the music box is turned, Bugs Bunny pops out. 14.5" tall. $30-45. TM & © Warner Bros. Inc.

Paddle ball, wood/rubber. Ace Novelty Co., Inc., 1994. The paddle is shaped like Bugs Bunny. 9.5" tall. $10-15. TM & © Warner Bros. Inc.

Bubble toy, plastic. Manufacturer unknown, 1997. The rocket can be filled with the bubble solution. Marvin the Martian is on top of a concealed bubble wand. 7" tall. $20-35. TM & © Warner Bros. Inc.

Telephone, plastic. Mattel, Inc., 1978. When the cord is pulled at the telephone base, the selected character will say a phrase. 10" tall. $30-45. TM & © Warner Bros. Inc.

Wind up toy, plastic. Knickerbocker Toy Co./Preschool, 1978. "Hoppers." When the knob on the side is wound, Road Runner will hop. 4.25" tall. $20-35. TM & © Warner Bros. Inc.

Skediddler, plastic. Mattel, Inc., 1969. Bugs Bunny's head, arms, and legs move back and forth when he is pushed along. 6" tall. $85-100. TM & © Warner Bros. Inc.

Tea set, porcelain. Manufacturer unknown, 1998. "Best fwiends tea set." Tweety is shown on a solid pink background. 13 pieces. $35-50. TM & © Warner Bros. Inc.

Tea set, plastic. Chilton Toys, 1995. "Looney Tunes play set." Bugs Bunny and friends are shown on a white background. When cold liquids are poured into the cups, they will change color. 6 pieces plus silverware. $15-20. TM & © Warner Bros. Inc.

Tea set, plastic. Tootsie Toy, 1996. "Looney Tunes tea party." Tweety is shown on a pink plaid background. 13 pieces plus silverware. $20-35. TM & © Warner Bros. Inc.

Tea set, plastic. Tootsie Toy, 1997. Caption: "'Toon party tea service set." Sylvester is shown on a green plaid background. 14 pieces plus silverware. $20-35. TM & © Warner Bros. Inc.

Doll, vinyl. Manufacturer unknown, 1995. "Looney Tunes classic original collector doll" series. Bugs Bunny. 12" tall. $15-20. TM & © Warner Bros. Inc.

Doll, vinyl. Manufacturer unknown, 1995. "Looney Tunes classic original collector doll" series. Taz. 7.5" tall. $15-20. TM & © Warner Bros. Inc.

Doll, vinyl. Manufacturer unknown, 1995. "Looney Tunes classic original collector doll" series. Sylvester. 9" tall. $15-20. TM & © Warner Bros. Inc.

Doll, vinyl. Manufacturer unknown, 1995. "Looney Tunes classic original collector doll" series. Daffy Duck. 9" tall. $15-20. TM & © Warner Bros. Inc.

Doll, vinyl. Manufacturer unknown, 1995. "Looney Tunes classic original collector doll" series. Tweety. 6.25" tall. $15-20. TM & © Warner Bros. Inc.

Doll, vinyl. Manufacturer unknown, 1995. "Looney Tunes classic original collector doll" series. Marvin the Martian. 8.5" tall. $15-20. TM & © Warner Bros. Inc.

Doll, vinyl. Manufacturer unknown, 1995. "Looney Tunes classic original collector doll" series. K-9. 7.5" tall. $20-35. TM & © Warner Bros. Inc.

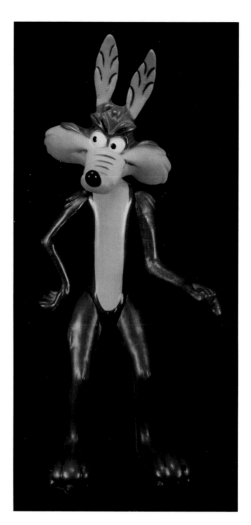

Doll, vinyl. R. Dakin & Company, 1968. Wile E. Coyote. 10.5" tall. $40-55. TM & © Warner Bros. Inc.

Doll, vinyl. R. Dakin & Company, 1968. Daffy Duck. 9" tall. $40-55. TM & © Warner Bros. Inc.

Toy, tin. Manufacturer unknown, 1992. Sylvester's truck. Caption: "Sylvester's bird catching service. Est. 1932. Officially sanctioned. Cat approved." 4.75" tall. $30-45. TM & © Warner Bros. Inc.

Doll, fuzzy material. Manufacturer unknown, 1988. Wile E. Coyote and Road Runner. Under 4.5" tall. $15-20 each. TM & © Warner Bros. Inc.

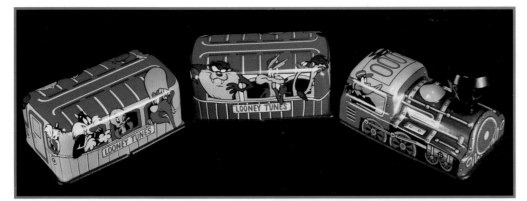

Train, tin. Manufacturer unknown, 1993. There is a wind-up mechanism on the side of the engine. Bugs Bunny and Daffy Duck are the train conductors. 2.25" tall. $40-55. TM & © Warner Bros. Inc.

Toy, tin. Manufacturer unknown, 1992. Wile E. Coyote's truck. Caption: "Wile E. Coyote's traveling gadget shoppe. Est. 1935. Manufacturer of anything a coyote ever needs." 4.75" tall. $30-45. TM & © Warner Bros. Inc.

Toy, tin. Manufacturer unknown, 1992. Bugs Bunny's truck. Caption: "B. Bunny, Greengrocer. Certified Best Overall. Farm fresh. Home delivery." 4.75" tall. $30-45. TM & © Warner Bros. Inc.

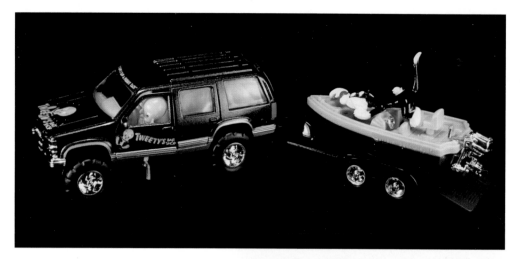

Toy, metal/plastic. Tootsie Toy, 1997. Tweety is shown driving a sport truck. Sylvester is trailing behind on a boat named "Suffrin' succotash!" 3" tall. $25-40 set. TM & © Warner Bros. Inc.

Toy, metal/plastic. Tootsie Toy, 1997. Taz is shown driving a sport truck. Bugs is trailing behind on a jet ski named "What's up, Doc?" 3" tall. $25-40 set. TM & © Warner Bros. Inc.

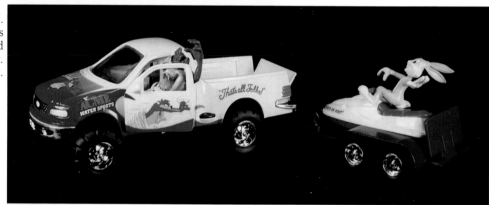

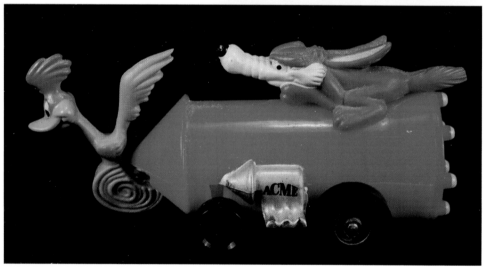

Toy, plastic. Manufacturer unknown, 1990. Wile E. Coyote is shown riding on top of an "ACME" rocket. 1.5" tall. $15-20. TM & © Warner Bros. Inc.

Toy, metal/plastic. Ertl Co., 1988. Road Runner is shown in an orange jeep. Caption: "Beep beep!" 2.5" tall. $25-40. TM & © Warner Bros. Inc.

Toy, metal/plastic. Ertl Co., 1988. Bugs Bunny is shown in an airplane. Caption: "What's up, Doc?" 2.5" tall. $20-35. TM & © Warner Bros. Inc.

Toy, metal/plastic. Ertl Co., 1988. Bugs Bunny is shown driving a red convertible. Caption: "What's up, Doc?" 2.5" tall. $20-35. TM & © Warner Bros. Inc.

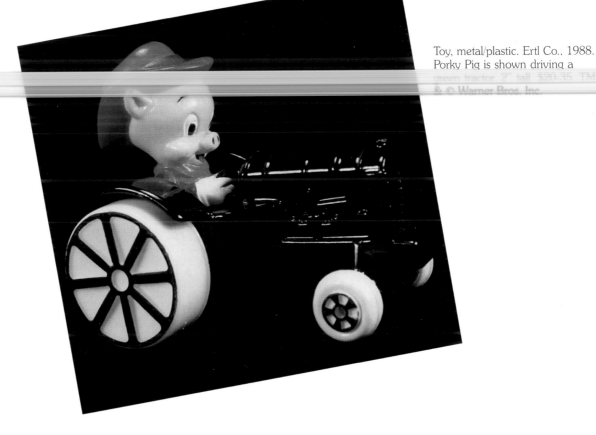

Toy, metal/plastic. Ertl Co., 1988. Porky Pig is shown driving a green tractor. 2" tall. $20-35. TM & © Warner Bros. Inc.

Toy, metal/plastic. Ertl Co., 1988. Daffy Duck is shown driving a fire truck. 1.75" tall. $20-35. TM & © Warner Bros. Inc.

Toy, metal/plastic. Ertl Co., 1988. Tweety is shown driving a blue convertible. Caption: "I tawt I taw a puddy tat!" 1.5" tall. $20-35. TM & © Warner Bros. Inc.

Toy, metal/plastic. Ertl Co., 1988. Sylvester is shown driving a yellow convertible. Caption: "Sufferin' succotash!" 2" tall. $20-35. TM & © Warner Bros. Inc.

Toy, metal/plastic. Matchbox International, Ltd., 1993. Wile E. Coyote is shown driving a white car. 1.75" tall. $20-35. TM & © Warner Bros. Inc.

Toy, metal/plastic. Matchbox International, Ltd., 1993. Road Runner is shown driving an orange car. 2.5" tall. $25-40. TM & © Warner Bros. Inc.

Toy, metal/plastic. Matchbox International, Ltd., 1993. Bugs Bunny is shown driving a white car with a carrot painted on the top. Caption: "Looney Tunes racing." 3" tall. $20-35. TM & © Warner Bros. Inc.

Toy, metal/plastic. Matchbox International, Ltd., 1993. Bugs Bunny is shown driving a white car with red and orange stripes. Caption: "Carrot plugs." 3" tall. $20-35. TM & © Warner Bros. Inc.

Toys   99

Toy, metal/plastic. Matchbox International, Ltd., 1993. Daffy Duck is shown driving a green and purple truck. Caption: "You're despicable!!!" 2" tall. $20-35. TM & © Warner Bros. Inc.

Toy, metal/plastic. Matchbox International, Ltd., 1995. Taz is shown driving a yellow race car. Caption: "Taz trans." 3" tall. $20-35. TM & © Warner Bros. Inc.

Toy, plastic. McDonald's promotion, 1989. Canada. "Looney Tunes" series. Complete set of four. Titled "Sylvester & Tweety Bird in Airplane." 2.5" tall. $15-20. TM & © Warner Bros. Inc.

Toy, plastic. McDonald's promotion, 1989. Canada. "Looney Tunes" series. Complete set of four. Titled "Daffy Duck in Car." 3" tall. $15-20. TM & © Warner Bros. Inc.

Toy, plastic. McDonald's promotion, 1989. Canada. "Looney Tunes" series. Complete set of four. Titled "Wile E. Coyote & Road Runner on a Handcart." 3.75" tall. $20-35. TM & © Warner Bros. Inc.

Toy, plastic. Arby's promotion, 1989. "Looney Tunes Car-Tunes" series. Complete set of six. Titled "Yosemite Sam Rockin' Frockin' Wagon." 2.25" tall. $5-10. TM & © Warner Bros. Inc.

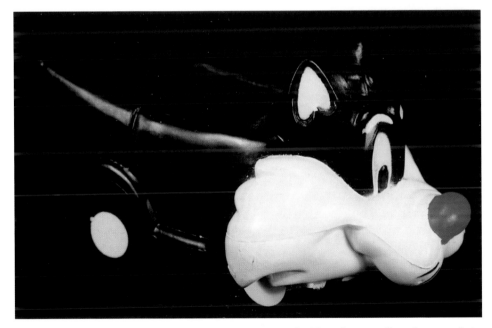

Toy, plastic. Arby's promotion, 1989. "Looney Tunes Car-Tunes" series. Complete set of six. Titled "Sylvester Cat-illac." 1.75" tall. $5-10. TM & © Warner Bros. Inc.

Toy, plastic. Arby's promotion,1989. "Looney Tunes Car-Tunes" series. Complete set of six. Titled "Road Runner Racer." 2" tall. $10-15. TM & © Warner Bros. Inc.

Toy, plastic. Arby's promotion, 1989. "Looney Tunes Car-Tunes" series. Complete set of six. Titled "Daffy Duck Dragster." 2" tall. $5-10. TM & © Warner Bros. Inc.

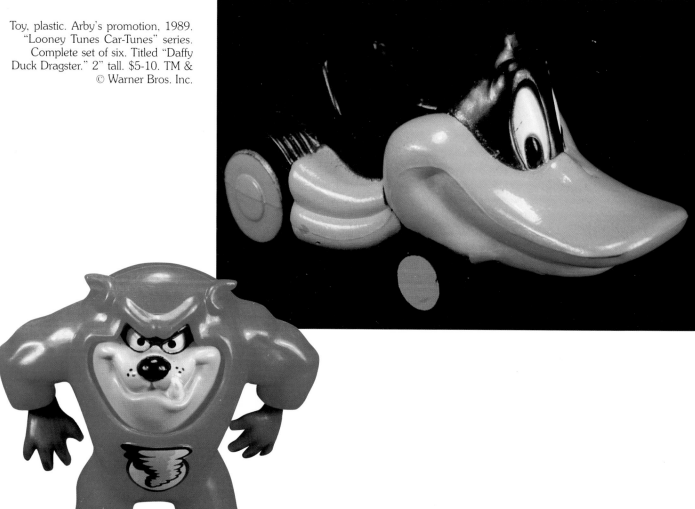

Toy, plastic. McDonald's promotion, 1991. "Super Heroes" series. Complete set of five. Titled "Tazmanian Devil as Taz-Flash." The costume snaps on and off. 2.5" tall. $10-15. TM & © Warner Bros. Inc.

Toy, plastic. McDonald's promotion, 1991. "Super Heroes" series. Complete set of five. Titled "Petunia Pig as Wonder·Pig." The costume snaps on and off. 2.75" tall. $10-15. TM & © Warner Bros. Inc.

Toy, plastic. McDonald's promotion, 1991. "Super Heroes" series. Complete set of five. Titled "Daffy Duck as Bat-Duck." The costume snaps on and off. 3" tall. $10-15. TM & © Warner Bros. Inc.

Toy, plastic. McDonald's promotion, 1991. "Super Heroes" series. Complete set of five. Titled "Bugs Bunny as Super Bugs." The costume snaps on and off. 3.5" tall. $10-15. TM & © Warner Bros. Inc.

Toy, plastic. McDonald's promotion, 1991. "Super Heroes" series. Complete set of five. Titled "Daffy in Bat-Duckmobile." Toy for children under the age of three. 2" tall. $15-20. TM & © Warner Bros. Inc.

Display, cardboard/plastic. McDonald's promotion, 1993. Titled "Looney Tunes Happy Meal." Caption: "Quack-'em-up punch-out fun on every box." 19" tall. $110-125. TM & © Warner Bros. Inc.

Box. McDonald's promotion, 1993. Caption: "Quack-up car chase happy meal punch-out playbox." 9.5" tall. $10-15. TM & © Warner Bros. Inc.

Toy, plastic. McDonald's promotion, 1993. "Looney Tunes Quack-Up Cars" series. Complete set of five. Titled "Taz in Tornado Tracker." 2.25" tall. $5-10. TM & © Warner Bros. Inc.

Toy, plastic. McDonald's promotion, 1993. "Looney Tunes Quack-Up Cars" series. Complete set of five. Titled "Porky's Ghost Catchers." 2.75" tall. $5-10. TM & © Warner Bros. Inc.

Toy, plastic. McDonald's promotion, 1993. "Looney Tunes Quack-Up Cars" series. Complete set of five. Titled "Daffy in Spittin' Sportster." 2" tall. $5-10. TM &© Warner Bros. Inc.

Toy, plastic. McDonald's promotion, 1993. "Looney Tunes Quack-Up Cars" series. Complete set of five. Titled "Bugs in Swingin' Sedan." Toy for children under the age of three. 2.25" tall. $10-15. TM & © Warner Bros. Inc.

Toy, plastic. McDonald's promotion, 1993. "Looney Tunes Quack-Up Cars" series. Complete set of five. Titled "Bugs in Super Stretch Limo." 2.25" tall. $5-10. TM & © Warner Bros. Inc.

Author's note: *An orange stretch limo was also manufactured. It is harder to find because it had limited distribution.*

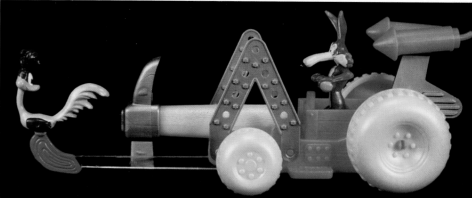

Action figures, plastic. Kinder, 1997. Germany. Wile E. Coyote rides in a vehicle that has a giant hammer attached to the front. As the vehicle moves forward, the hammer goes up and down. 3.25" tall. $45-60. TM & © Warner Bros. Inc.

Toy, plastic. McDonald's promotion, 1994. "Happy Birthday" series. Bugs Bunny flattens Daffy Duck's head between a pair of cymbals. This car attaches to a 15-piece train. 4" tall. $10-15. TM & © Warner Bros. Inc.

Action figures, plastic. Playmates, 1997. Bugs Bunny and Taz. Titled *Dr. Devil and Mr. Hare.* Kit includes: one hammer, paint can, brush, and glasses. Bugs Bunny: 5" tall. Taz: 3" tall. $30-45 set. TM & © Warner Bros. Inc.

Action figures, plastic. Playmates, 1997. Road Runner and Wile E. Coyote. Titled *Gee Whiz-z-z-z-z-z.* Kit includes: one flight suit, back pack, and artillery. Road Runner: 3" tall. Wile E. Coyote: 4" tall. $35-50 set. TM & © Warner Bros. Inc.

Action figures, plastic. Playmates, 1997. Daffy Duck and Marvin the Martian. Titled *"Duck Dodgers in the 24 1/2th Century."* Kit includes: two pistols, and flags. Daffy Duck: 4" tall. Marvin the Martian: 3.25" tall. $30-45 set. TM & © Warner Bros. Inc.

Action figure, plastic. Tyco Industries, Ltd. Road Runner. Caption: "Road Runner speeds away in a cloud of dust!" 4.75" tall. $20-35. TM & © Warner Bros. Inc.

Action figures, plastic. Playmates, 1997. Bugs Bunny and Gus Gorilla. Titled *"Baseball Bugs."* Kit includes: one baseball. The bat moves back and forth when the lever in Gus' back is turned. Bugs Bunny: 4" tall. Gus-House Gorilla: 6" tall. $35-50 set. TM & © Warner Bros. Inc.

Slide puzzle. American Publishing, Corp., 1979. Bugs Bunny is shown holding a basket full of carrots. Approximately 4" tall. $10-15. TM & © Warner Bros. Inc.

Slide puzzle. American Publishing, Corp., 1979. Bugs Bunny is shown holding Daffy Duck's mouth shut. Approximately 4" tall. $10-15. TM & © Warner Bros. Inc.

Puzzle. Whitman/Guild-Western Publishing Company, Inc., 1977. Bugs Bunny and friends are riding on a roller coaster. 125 interlocking pieces. $15-20. TM & © Warner Bros. Inc.

Puzzle. Whitman/Western Publishing Company, Inc., 1975. Sylvester is shown with his hand in Tweety's bird cage. 99 interlocking pieces. $10-15. TM &©Warner Bros. Inc.

Puzzle. Western Publishing Company, Inc., 1981. Caption: "A Looney Tunes family portrait featuring over 100 favorite characters." 300 pieces. $15-20. TM & © Warner Bros. Inc.

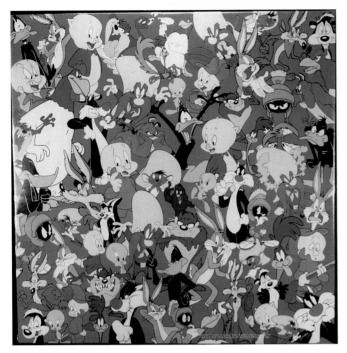

Puzzle. Springbok by Hallmark Cards, Inc., 1994. Looney Tunes characters are shown on a green background. 500 pieces. $15-20. TM & © Warner Bros. Inc.

Puzzle. Golden/Western Publishing Company, Inc., 1983. Wile E. Coyote is shown skiing down a wooden slope. 100 pieces. $10-15. TM & © Warner Bros. Inc.

Puzzle. Whitman/Western Publishing Company, Inc., 1982. Wile E. Coyote is shown posing as a photographer. 100 pieces. $10-15. TM & © Warner Bros. Inc.

Puzzle. Golden/Western Publishing Company, Inc., 1983. Bugs Bunny and friends are shown depicting nursery rhymes. 100 pieces. $5-10. TM & © Warner Bros. Inc.

Puzzle.Golden/Western Publishing, Company, Inc., 1984. Bugs Bunny is shown practicing how to make knots. 100 pieces. $5-10. TM & © Warner Bros. Inc.

Puzzle.Whitman/Western Publishing Company, Inc., 1976. Frame-Tray puzzle. Bugs Bunny and Yosemite Sam are shown on a ship. 12 pieces. $5-10. TM & © Warner Bros. Inc.

Puzzle.The Rainbow Works, 1990. Bugs Bunny and friends are shown at a costume party. 63 pieces. $5-10. TM & © Warner Bros. Inc.

Puzzle. Golden/Western Publishing Company, Inc., 1985. Frame-Tray puzzle. Bugs Bunny and friends are shown on a farm. 22 pieces. $5-10. TM & © Warner Bros. Inc.

Puzzle. Landoll's, Inc., 1997. My favorite puzzle. Bugs Bunny. Caption: "Puzzling, ain't it?" 24 pieces. $5-10. TM & © Warner Bros. Inc.

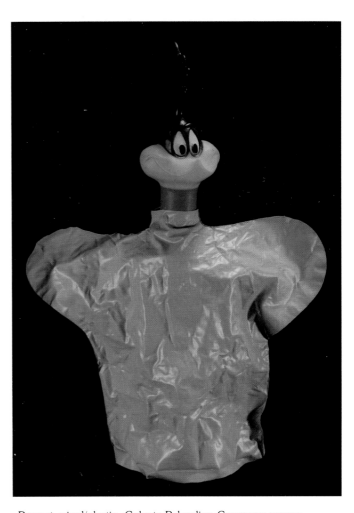

Puppet, vinyl/plastic. Colgate-Polmolive Company promotion, N/A. Road Runner. 10.5" tall. $25-40. TM & © Warner Bros. Inc.

Finger puppet, vinyl/fabric. Manufacturer unknown, 1978. Tweety. 3.5" tall. $10-15. TM & © Warner Bros. Inc.

Puppet, vinyl/plastic. Colgate-Polmolive Company promotion, N/A. Wile E. Coyote. 10" tall. $20-35. TM & © Warner Bros. Inc.

Toy, plush. Steiff, 1997. Fully jointed Bugs Bunny has the Steiff "button-in-ear" trademark. Limited Edition size of 2,500. First in series. 12" tall. $375-390. TM & © Warner Bros. Inc.

Puppet, plush. The 24K Company. Special Effects division of Mighty Star, Inc., 1993. Bugs Bunny. 14" tall. $10-15. TM & © Warner Bros. Inc.

Toys, plush. Steiff, 1998. Fully jointed Sylvester and Tweety have the Steiff "button-in-ear" trademark. Limited Edition size of 2,500. Second in series. Under 13" tall. $565-580 set. TM & © Warner Bros. Inc.

Toy, plush. Tyco Industries, Ltd., 1994. Talking Road Runner. When his belly is squeezed, he says one of three phrases. For example: "Beep beep." 15" tall. $35-50. TM & © Warner Bros. Inc.

Toys, plush. Play-By-Play, 1998. Talking Tweety and Sylvester. When their hands are squeezed, they talk to each other. For example: "Oooh, I taut I taw a puddy tat." Under 15.5" tall. $65-80 set. TM & © Warner Bros. Inc.

Toys, plush. Play-By-Play, 1998. Talking Daffy Duck and Bugs Bunny. When their hands are squeezed, they talk to each other. For example: "Eh, What's up, Duck?" Under 15.5" tall. $65-80 set. TM & © Warner Bros. Inc.

Toy, plush. Fun Farm, 1978. Tweety has appliquéd features. 8" tall. $20-35. TM & © Warner Bros. Inc.

Toy, plush. Mattel, Inc., 1964. When the cord is pulled, Bugs Bunny says multiple phrases. 20" tall. $65-80. TM & © Warner Bros. Inc.

Toy, plush. Tyco Playtime, Inc., 1994. Wile E. Coyote. 12" tall. $20-35. TM & © Warner Bros. Inc.

Toy, plush. R. Dakin & Co., 1975. Porky Pig has appliquéd features. 7" tall. $20-35. TM & © Warner Bros. Inc.

Toy, plush. Mighty Star, Ltd., 1971. Wile E. Coyote. 18" tall. $25-40. TM & © Warner Bros. Inc.

Toy, plush. Mighty Star, Ltd., 1971. Bugs Bunny is shown wearing a yellow button. Caption: "Happy Easter." 16" tall. $25-40. TM & © Warner Bros. Inc.

Toy, plush. Mighty Star, Ltd., 1971. Road Runner. 12.5" tall. $30-45. TM & © Warner Bros. Inc.

Toy, plush. Applause, Inc., 1994. Taz and She-devil are dressed up in wedding attire. 7" tall. $40-55 set. TM & © Warner Bros. Inc.

Toy, plush. Ace a subsidiary of Play-By-Play, 1997. Speedy Gonzales. 12.5" tall. $15-20. TM & © Warner Bros. Inc.

Pencil sharpener. Manufacturer unknown, 1977. Tweety is shown on top of a pencil sharpener. 3.5" tall. $10-15. TM & © Warner Bros. Inc.

Stationery

Stapler, plastic. Janex Corp., 1975. Bugs Bunny. Caption: "Eh, Clip it, Doc!" Battery operated. 7.5" tall. $30-45. TM & © Warner Bros. Inc.

Pencils. Dixon Ticonderoga Company, 1996. Four pencils were packaged with a free punch out bookmark. Various characters were produced. Tweety. One size. $5-10. TM & © Warner Bros. Inc.

Scissors, plastic/metal. Manufacturer unknown, 1997. Bugs Bunny. 10"tall. $20-35. TM & © Warner Bros. Inc.

Pencil holder, plastic. Janex Corp., 1975. Pencils can be stored in either the log or grass sections around Bugs Bunny. 5.5" tall. $15-20. TM & © Warner Bros. Inc.

Rubber Stamp, wood/rubber. Rubber Stampede, 1992. Road Runner. 2.25" tall. $10-15. TM & © Warner Bros. Inc.

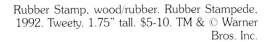
Rubber Stamp, wood/rubber. Rubber Stampede, 1992. Tweety. 1.75" tall. $5-10. TM & © Warner Bros. Inc.

Stamper, plastic. Ha Ha Ha a division of Sunkisses Hawaii, Ltd., 1996. "Looney Tunes Blues" series. Taz, Tweety, Bugs Bunny, and Marvin the Martian stand on top of concealed ink pads. 3.5" tall. $10-15 each. TM & © Warner Bros. Inc.

3-D Card. Popshots, Inc., N/A. Daffy Duck, Marvin the Martian, and Porky Pig are shown on a planet. Caption: "Have a blast. . . on y-your- b-birth-b-bir-birthday!" 5.25"tall. $15-20. TM & © Warner Bros. Inc.

3-D Card. Popshots, Inc., N/A. Taz scares Bugs Bunny and friends when he jumps out of a cake. Caption: "Happy Birthday! You devil." 5.25" tall. $15-20. TM & © Warner Bros. Inc.

3-D Card. Popshots, Inc., N/A. Bugs Bunny plays the piano for his friends. Caption: "Happy Birthday to you! And many happy re...r...retu...re....r...re...retu...salutations!" 5.25" tall. $15-20. TM & © Warner Bros. Inc.

3-D Card. Popshots, Inc., N/A. Sylvester watches over Tweety in his nest. Caption: "Thuprise!! Happy Birthday." 5.25" tall. $15-20. TM & © Warner Bros. Inc.

3-D Card. Popshots, Inc., N/A. Pepé Le Pew is holding a bouquet of roses. Caption: "Happee Birzday Ma Cherie! 7.25" tall. $20-35. TM & © Warner Bros. Inc.

3-D Card. Popshots, Inc., N/A. Wile E. Coyote has set a birthday cake trap for Road Runner. Caption: "Happy Birthday. Happious Birthdayicus." 5.25" tall. $20-35. TM & © Warner Bros. Inc.

3-D Card. Popshots, Inc., N/A. Pepé Le Pew is shown holding Penelope. Caption: "Love... She is Blind. No?" 5.25" tall. $20-35. TM & © Warner Bros. Inc.

Memo pad. Manufacturer unknown, 1993. This magnetic memo pad holder came with loose Taz sheets of paper. 6.25" tall. $10-15. TM & © Warner Bros. Inc.

Memo pad. Conimar Corp., 1997. This magnetic memo pad came with a Wile E. Coyote magnet. Memo pad: 9.5" tall. $5-10. Magnet: 3.25" tall. $5-10. TM & © Warner Bros. Inc.

Postage stamps. United States Postal Service, 1997. Bugs Bunny is shown on 32 cent stamps in commemoration of being an American icon. First in series. Self-adhesive. One size. $5-10 sheet. TM & © Warner Bros. Inc.

Postage stamps. United States Postal Service, 1998. Sylvester and Tweety are shown on 32 cent stamps in commemoration of being American icons. Second in series. Self-adhesive. One size. $5-10 sheet. TM & © Warner Bros. Inc.

Stationery. Hallmark Cards, Inc., 1997. Various Looney Tunes designs. Complete with nine blank notes, ten envelopes, and two sticker sheets. 6.5" tall. $15-20. TM & © Warner Bros. Inc.

Valentine's Day cards. Hallmark Cards, Inc., 1997. Bugs Bunny and friends are shown on each card. Complete with 30 Valentines. 8.75" tall. $5-10. TM & © Warner Bros. Inc.

Valentine's Day cards/ stickers. Mello Smello, 1996. Complete with 32 sticker Valentine cards, one tote box, and two cut out teacher cards. 10.75" tall. $10-15. TM & © Warner Bros. Inc.

Valentine's Day cards. Cleo, Inc., 1997. "Static cling Valentine kit." The box contains 30 Looney Tunes Valentines. 9.25" tall. $5-10. TM & © Warner Bros. Inc.

Sticker. Manufacturer unknown, 1997. Road Runner is shown on the center of a one dollar bill. Various Looney Tunes characters were available on different denominations. 2.5" tall. $10-15. TM & © Warner Bros. Inc.

Sticker book. Golden/Western Publishing Co., Inc., 1990. Bugs Bunny is shown walking in the woods with Daffy Duck. 12" tall. $15-20. TM & © Warner Bros. Inc.

Books

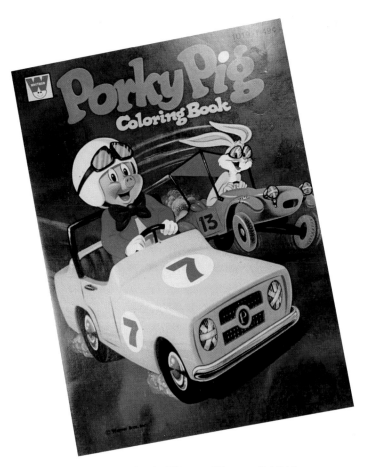

Activity book. Whitman/Western Publishing Company, 1972. *Porky Pig Coloring Book*. Porky Pig is shown driving a race car. 11" tall. $10-15. TM & © Warner Bros. Inc.

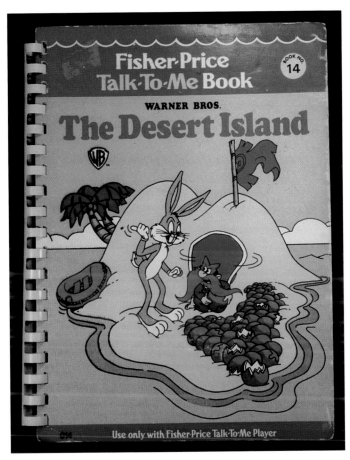

Book, soft cover. Phonorecords of sound recordings/Fisher-Price Toys, 1978. "Fisher-Price Talk-To-Me" book. *The Desert Island* written by Jerry Harrison, illustrated by Stan Smith, and recorded voices by Mel Blanc. The small record attached to each page can only be used with a "Fisher-Price Talk-To-Me" player. 11.5" tall. $20-35. TM & © Warner Bros. Inc.

Activity book. Whitman/Western Publishing Company, 1981. *Porky Pig Coloring Book*. Porky Pig is shown as a waiter. 11" tall. $5-10. TM & © Warner Bros. Inc.

Activity book. Whitman/Western Publishing Company, 1980. *Tweety & Sylvester Color Book. Cat Nap Confusion.* Sylvester is shown eating a horseradish sandwich. 11" tall. $5-10. TM & © Warner Bros. Inc.

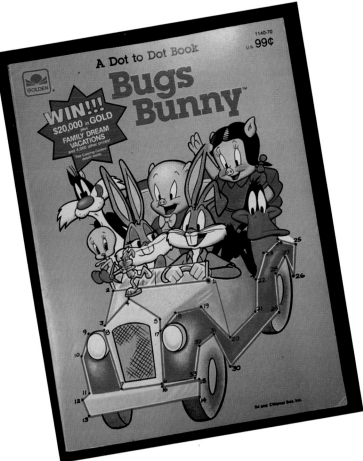

Activity book. Golden/Western Publishing Company, 1984. *Bugs Bunny. A Dot to Dot Book.* Bugs Bunny is shown driving his friends in a car. 11" tall. $5-10. TM & © Warner Bros. Inc.

Book, hard cover. Intervisual Books, Inc., 1996. A Looney Tunes pop-up book. *Looney Love.* Designed by Willabel L. Tong. Paper engineered by Jose R. Seminario. Pencils by Allen Helbig. Painting by Eric Binder and Judi Cassell. 4.25" tall. $20-35. TM & © Warner Bros. Inc.

Book, hard cover. Intervisual Books, Inc., 1996. A Looney Tunes pop-up book. *Keep Smiling!* Designed by Willabel L. Tong. Paper engineered by Renee Jablow. Pencils by Allen Helbig. Painting by Eric Binder and Judi Cassell. 4.25" tall. $15-20. TM & © Warner Bros. Inc.

Book, soft cover. Golden/Western Publishing Company, Inc., 1980. A Golden Shape Book. *Bugs Bunny and Friends* by Rebecca A. Ecklund and Bob Ottum. Illustrated by Lee Holley and Milli Jancar. 8" tall. $5-10. TM & © Warner Bros. Inc.

Book, hard cover. Landoll, Inc., 1996. A Looney Tunes pop-up book. *Daffy Duck's Family Tree*. Author unknown. 8" tall. $15-20. TM & © Warner Bros. Inc.

Book, soft cover. Western Publishing Company, Inc., 1977. A Golden Look-Look Book. *Bugs Bunny's Space Carrot* by Seymour Reit. Pictures by Ralph Heimdahl and William Lorencz. 8.25" tall. $5-10. TM & © Warner Bros. Inc.

Book, soft cover. Western Publishing Company, Inc., 1978. A Golden Look-Look Book. *Bugs Bunny Goes to the Dentist* by Seymour Reit. Pictures by Lou Cunette. 8.25" tall. $5-10. TM & © Warner Bros. Inc.

Book, soft cover. Western Publishing Company, Inc., 1977. A Golden Look-Look Book. *Tweety and Sylvester Birds of a Feather* by Seymour Reit. Pictures by Lou Cunette. 8.25" tall. $5-10. TM & © Warner Bros. Inc.

Book, hard cover. Whitman Publishing
Company, 1948. Story Hour series. *Bugs
Bunny's Adventures*. Author unknown. 6.5" tall.
$15-20. TM & © Warner Bros. Inc.

Book, hard cover. Golden Press, Inc., 1951. A
Little Golden Book. *Bugs Bunny and the Indians*
told by Annie North Bedford. Pictures by
Richmond I. Kelsey and Tom McKimson. 8" tall.
$20-35. TM & © Warner Bros. Inc.

Book, hard cover. Golden Press, Inc., 1949. A Little
Golden Book. *Bugs Bunny* by Warner Bros. Cartoons,
Inc. Pictures by Warner Bros. Cartoons, Inc. Adapted by
Tom McKimson and Al Dempster. 8" tall. $20-35. TM &
© Warner Bros. Inc.

Book, hard cover. Simon and Schuster, 1950. A Little Golden Book. *Bugs Bunny's Birthday* by Warner Bros. Cartoon, Inc. Adapted by Elizabeth Beecher, Ralph Heimdahl, and Al Dempster. 8" tall. $20-35. TM & © Warner Bros. Inc.

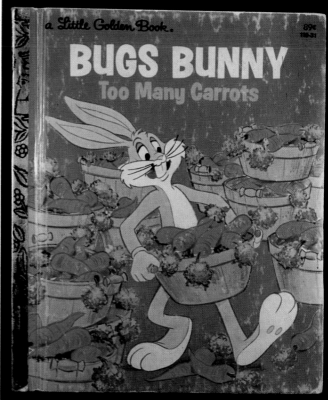

Book, hard cover. Golden Press/Western Publishing Company, Inc., 1976. A Little Golden Book. *Bugs Bunny Too Many Carrots* by Jean Lewis. Illustrated by Peter Alvarado and Bob Totten. 8" tall. $10-15. TM & © Warner Bros. Inc.

Book, hard cover. Whitman/Western Publishing Company, Inc., 1968. A Big Little Book. *The Road Runner. The Super Beep-Catcher* by Carl Fallberg. 5" tall. $20-35. TM & © Warner Bros. Inc.

Book, soft cover. Whitman/Western Publishing Company, Inc., 1974. A Big Little Book. *Bugs Bunny and Klondike Gold*. Author unknown. 4.75" tall. $15-20. TM & © Warner Bros. Inc.

Book, hard cover. Golden Book/Western Publishing Company, Inc., 1987. A Golden Tell-A-Tale Book. *Tweety and Sylvester: A Visit to the Vet* by Jean Lewis. Illustrated by Joe Messerli. 6.5" tall. $10-15. TM & © Warner Bros. Inc.

Book, hard cover. Golden Book/Western Publishing Company, Inc., 1977. A Golden Tell-A-Tale Book. *Daffy Duck: Space Creature* by Gina Ingoglia. Pictures by Darrell Baker. 6.5" tall. $10-15. TM & © Warner Bros. Inc.

Book, hard cover. Golden Book/Western Publishing Company, Inc., 1985. A Golden Tell-A-Tale Book. *No Sit-Ups for Porky Pig* by Gina Ingoglia. Illustrated by Joe Messerli. 6.5" tall. $10-15. TM & © Warner Bros. Inc.

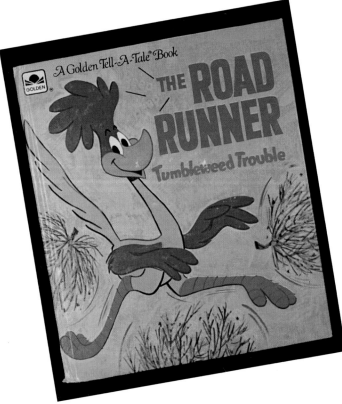

Book, hard cover. Golden Book/Western Publishing Company, Inc., 1986. A Golden Tell-A-Tale Book. *Bugs Bunny Rides Again* by Jean Lewis. Illustrated by Joe Messerli. 6.5" tall. $10-15. TM & © Warner Bros. Inc.

Book, hard cover. Golden Book/Western Publishing Company, Inc., 1971. A Golden Tell-A-Tale Book. *The Road Runner Tumbleweed Trouble* by Jack Woolgar. Illustrated by Leon Jason Studio. 6.5" tall. $15-20. TM & © Warner Bros. Inc.

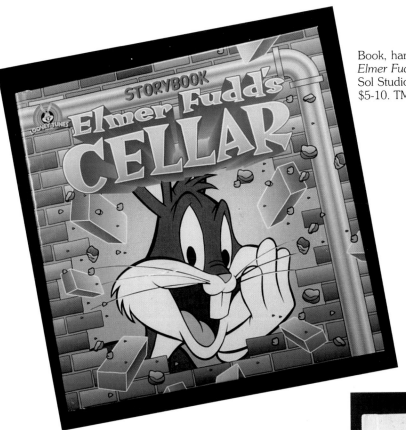

Book, hard cover. Landoll, Inc., 1997. Storybook. *Elmer Fudd's Cellar* by Julie McNally. Illustrated by Sol Studios, Argentina, and Landoll, Inc. 8.5" tall. $5-10. TM & © Warner Bros. Inc.

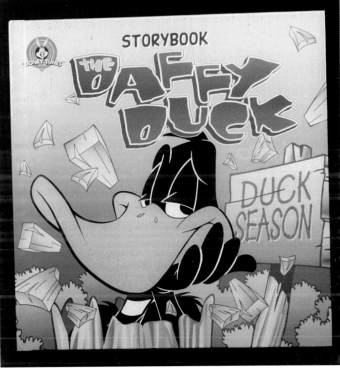

Book, hard cover. Landoll, Inc., 1997. Storybook. *The Daffy Duck* by Julie McNally and Tim Cahill. Illustrated by Sol Studios, Argentina, and Landoll, Inc. 8.5" tall. $5-10. TM & © Warner Bros. Inc.

Book, hard cover. Landoll, Inc., 1997. Storybook. *Full Moon Feline* by Charles Carney. Illustrated by Sol Studios, Argentina, and Landoll, Inc. 8.5" tall. $5-10. TM & © Warner Bros. Inc.

Book, hard cover. Landoll, Inc., 1997. Storybook. *The Wily Coyote* by Charles Carney. Adapted from stories by Chuck Jones and Michael Maltese. Illustrated by Sol Studios, Argentina and Landoll, Inc. 8.5" tall. $5-10. TM & © Warner Bros. Inc.

Comic book, soft cover. March of Comics/ Western Publishing Company, Inc., 1969. *Daffy Duck.* Buster Brown promotional comic. 6.75" tall. $15-20. TM & © Warner Bros. Inc.

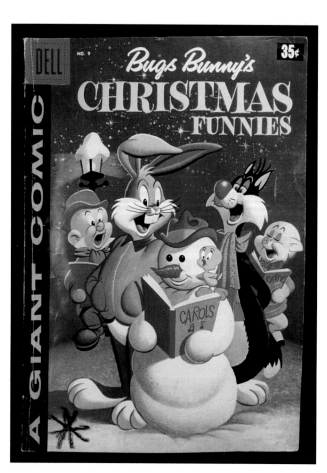

Comic book, soft cover. Dell Publishing Company, 1959. *A Giant Comic. Bugs Bunny's Christmas Funnies.* Issue #9. 10.25" tall. $20-35. TM & © Warner Bros. Inc.

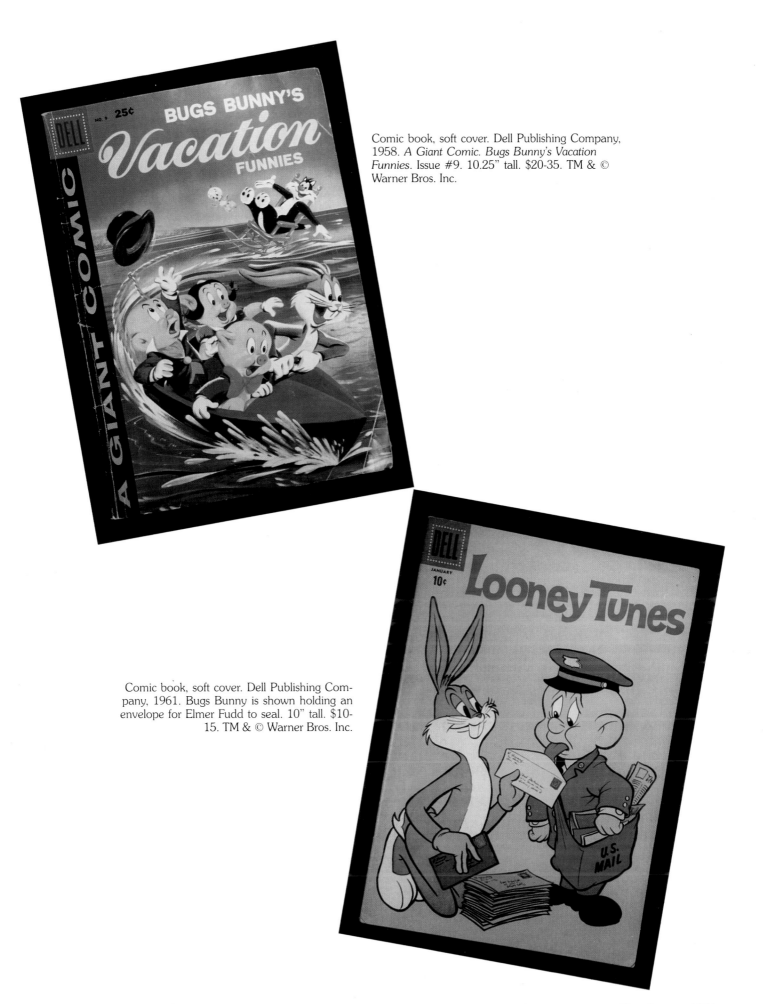

Comic book, soft cover. Dell Publishing Company, 1958. *A Giant Comic. Bugs Bunny's Vacation Funnies*. Issue #9. 10.25" tall. $20-35. TM & © Warner Bros. Inc.

Comic book, soft cover. Dell Publishing Company, 1961. Bugs Bunny is shown holding an envelope for Elmer Fudd to seal. 10" tall. $10-15. TM & © Warner Bros. Inc.

Gingerbread house, ceramic. Manufacturer unknown, 1997. Second in series. Granny welcomes you to a gingerbread house that lights up. 7" tall. $55-70. TM & © Warner Bros. Inc.

Teapot, ceramic. Manufacturer unknown, 1997. Tweety is shown putting a cherry on top of Sylvester's head. 9" tall. $60-75. TM & © Warner Bros. Inc.

Salt and pepper shakers, ceramic. Manufacturer unknown, 1997. Tweety and Sylvester are in the shape of gingerbread cookies. Under 4.75" tall. $20-35 set. TM & © Warner Bros. Inc.

Salt and pepper shakers, ceramic. Certified International Corp., 1993. Bugs Bunny and Taz are dressed in Santa outfits. Bugs Bunny: 5.5" tall. Taz: 4.5" tall. $20-35 set. TM & © Warner Bros. Inc.

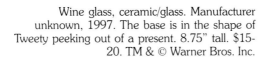

Wine glass, ceramic/glass. Manufacturer unknown, 1997. The base is in the shape of Tweety peeking out of a present. 8.75" tall. $15-20. TM & © Warner Bros. Inc.

Container, tin. Manufacturer unknown, 1994. Bugs is dressed like santa. 6.5" in diameter. $10-15. TM & © Warner Bros. Inc.

Candy container, tin. Jacobs Suchard, Inc., 1990. Brach's promotion commemorating Bugs Bunny's 50th birthday. The container originally had Bugs Bunny & Friends jellies. Caption: "Happy holidays." 6.25" tall. $10-15. TM & © Warner Bros. Inc.

Nutcracker, wood/resin. Midwest of Cannon Falls, 1996. Marvin the Martian has a lever concealed in his red shirt which controls his jaw. 8" tall. $100-115. TM & © Warner Bros. Inc.

Doll, clothique/fabric. Possible Dreams, Ltd., 1995. "The Clothique Looney Tunes" collection. Titled "Sylvester's Holiday High Jinks." Sylvester is dressed like Santa so that he can kidnap Tweety. 9" tall. $85-100. TM & © Warner Bros. Inc.

Doll, clothique/fabric. Possible Dreams, Ltd., 1995. "The Clothique Looney Tunes" collection. Titled "Yosemite Sam's Rootin' Tootin' Christmas." Yosemite Sam is wearing a sombrero decorated with Christmas lights. 8.5" tall. $75-90. TM & © Warner Bros. Inc.

Doll, clothique/fabric. Possible Dreams, Ltd., 1995. "The Clothique Looney Tunes" collection. Titled "Merry Master of Ceremonies." Elmer Fudd is shown announcing a list of contestants. 11" tall. $75-90. TM & © Warner Bros. Inc.

Doll, clothique/fabric. Possible Dreams, Ltd., 1995. "The Clothique Looney Tunes" collection. Titled "Selfish Elfish Daffy Duck." Daffy Duck is shown putting his name on all the presents. 8.5" tall. $75-90. TM & © Warner Bros. Inc.

Doll, clothique/fabric. Possible Dreams, Ltd., 1995. "The Clothique Looney Tunes" collection. Titled "Tasmanian Rhapsody." Taz is eating a book entitled *Tasteful Christmas Carols*. 8.5" tall. $75-90. TM & © Warner Bros. Inc.

Bank, plastic. Russell Stover Candies, 1997. Bugs Bunny is shown in front of a snow covered candy shop. This originally came with individually foil-wrapped milk chocolate characters. Caption: "Candy kitchen." 5" tall. $15-20. TM & © Warner Bros. Inc.

Box. Russell Stover Candies, 1997. The box originally contained an assortment of chocolates. 4.5" tall. $5-10. TM & © Warner Bros. Inc.

Music box, plastic. Matrix Industries, Ltd., 1996. Titled "Up on the Roof Top." Taz and She-devil are shown skating in front of a gingerbread house. 9" tall. $135-150. TM & © Warner Bros. Inc.

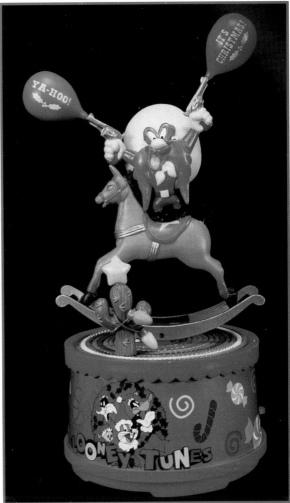

Music box, plastic. Matrix Industries, Ltd., 1996. Titled "Rocking Ranger." Yosemite Sam is shown riding on a rocking horse. 7" tall. $50-65. TM & © Warner Bros. Inc.

Music box, plastic. Matrix Industries, Ltd., 1996. Titled "Holiday on Ice." Daffy Duck is shown on skis. 7" tall. $50-65. TM & © Warner Bros. Inc.

Tree topper, clothique/resin. Manufacturer unknown, 1997. Marvin the Martian is made to adorn the top of a tree. 9" tall. $35-50. TM & © Warner Bros. Inc.

Christmas lights, plastic. Minami International Corp., 1997. "Ten light holiday fun set." Bugs Bunny and friends are shown. Under 4" tall. $20-35. TM & © Warner Bros. Inc.

Toy, plush. McDonalds promotion, 1992. Canada. Bugs Bunny is shown wearing a red and green scarf. 12" tall. $25-40. TM & © Warner Bros. Inc.

Toy, plush. McDonalds promotion, 1992. Canada. Sylvester is shown wearing a red and white striped shirt. 9" tall. $25-40. TM & © Warner Bros. Inc.

Toy, plush. McDonalds promotion, 1992. Canada. Taz is shown wearing a red cap. 9" tall. $25-40. TM & © Warner Bros. Inc.

Ornament/candy container, tin. Russell Stover Candies, 1997. Bugs Bunny is shown painting a Daffy Duck toy. 5.5" tall. $10-15. TM & © Warner Bros. Inc.

Ornament/candy container, tin. Russell Stover Candies, 1997. Road Runner is shown standing in front of a Christmas tree. 5.5" tall. $15-20. TM & © Warner Bros. Inc.

Ornament, resin. Manufacturer unknown, 1997. Marvin the Martian trails behind K-9 in a saucer sled. Complete with stand. 6" tall. $35-50 set. TM & © Warner Bros. Inc.

Ornament, resin. Midwest of Cannon Falls, 1997. Bugs Bunny is shown skiing. 3" tall. $20-35. TM & © Warner Bros. Inc.

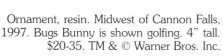

Ornament, resin. Midwest of Cannon Falls, 1997. Bugs Bunny is shown golfing. 4" tall. $20-35. TM & © Warner Bros. Inc.

Ornament, resin. Manufacturer unknown, 1997. Pepé Le Pew and Penelope are shown holding a gold heart. Caption: "Our first Christmas." 3" tall. $25-40. TM & © Warner Bros. Inc.

Ornament, plastic. Hallmark Cards, Inc., 1996. Foghorn Leghorn and Henery Hawk. Set of two ornaments. Celebrating 50 years. Sculpted by Robert Chad. Foghorn Leghorn: 3.5" tall. Henery Hawk: 1.25" tall. $35-50 set. TM & © Warner Bros. Inc.

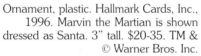

Ornament, plastic. Hallmark Cards, Inc., 1996. Marvin the Martian is shown dressed as Santa. 3" tall. $20-35. TM & © Warner Bros. Inc.

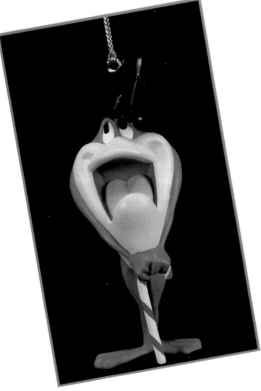

Ornament, plastic. Hallmark Cards, Inc., 1997. Michigan J. Frog is shown dancing with a candy cane. Sculpted by Robert Chad. 3.25" tall. $25-40. TM & © Warner Bros. Inc.

Ornament, plastic. Hallmark Cards, Inc., 1997. Light and motion ornament. Taz is shown decorating a tree. Sculpted by Robert Chad 4.5" tall. $50-65. TM & © Warner Bros. Inc.

Ornament, plastic. Matrix Industries, Ltd., 1995. Solar ornament. Bugs Bunny is shown with a carrot decorated Christmas tree. 4.5" tall. $35-50. TM & © Warner Bros. Inc.

Ornament, plastic. Matrix Industries, Ltd., 1997. Taz is shown wearing a top hat. 2.5" tall. $20-35. TM & © Warner Bros. Inc.

Ornament, plastic. Matrix Industries, Ltd., 1997. Bugs Bunny is shown laying on top of a television set. 4.5" tall. $20-35. TM & © Warner Bros. Inc.

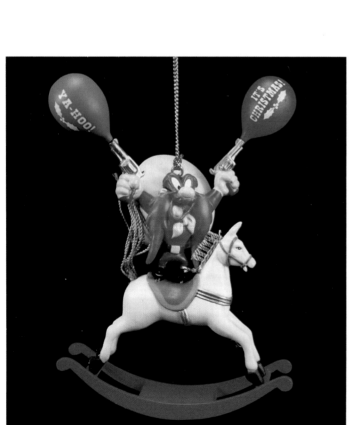

Ornament, plastic. Matrix Industries, Ltd., 1997. Yosemite Sam is shown riding a carrousel horse. 4.5" tall. $20-35. TM & © Warner Bros. Inc.

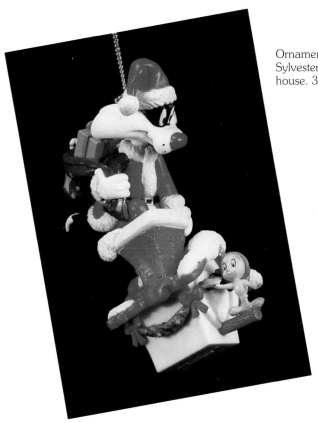

Ornament, plastic. Matrix Industries, Ltd., 1997. Sylvester is shown sneaking into Tweety's bird house. 3.5" tall. $25-40. TM & © Warner Bros. Inc.

Ornament, plastic. Matrix Industries, Ltd., 1997. Taz is shown sitting on top of a mailbox. 3.25" tall. $20-35. TM & © Warner Bros. Inc.

Ornament, plastic. Matrix Industries, Ltd., 1997. Daffy Duck is shown on top of a football. 3.5" tall. $20-35. TM & © Warner Bros. Inc.

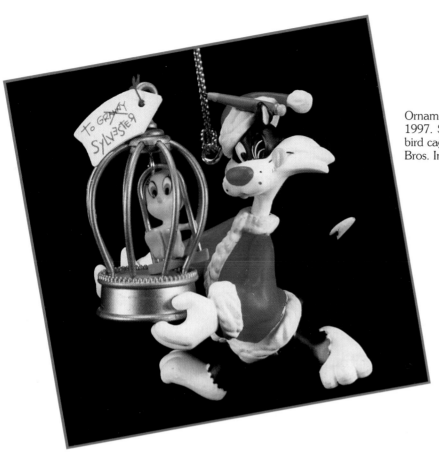

Ornament, plastic. Matrix Industries, Ltd., 1997. Sylvester is shown holding Tweety's bird cage. 3" tall. $25-40. TM & © Warner Bros. Inc.

Ornament, plastic. Matrix Industries, Ltd., 1997. Road Runner is shown delivering the mail. 3" tall. $25-40. TM & © Warner Bros. Inc.

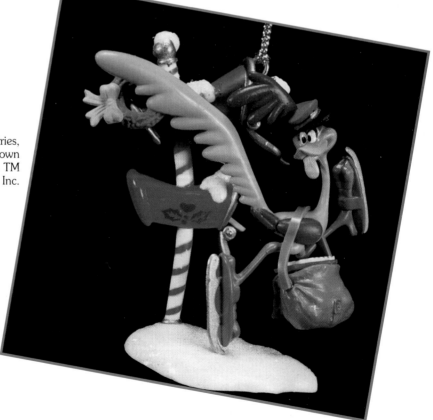

Ornament, plastic. Matrix Industries, Ltd., 1997. She-devil is shown on top of a heart shaped candy cane. 4.5" tall. $25-40. TM & © Warner Bros. Inc.

Ornament, plastic. Matrix Industries, Ltd., 1997. Marvin the Martian is shown riding a carrousel horse. 4" tall. $20-35. TM & © Warner Bros. Inc.

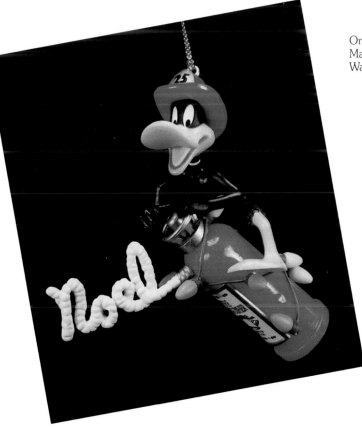

Ornament, plastic. Matrix Industries, Ltd., 1997. Daffy Duck is shown on top of a fire estinguisher. Caption: "Noel." 4" tall. $20-35. TM & © Warner Bros. Inc.

Ornament, plastic. Matrix Industries, Ltd., 1997. Bugs Bunny is shown in a Santa sleigh. Caption: "Good Children List." 3.5" tall. $20-35. TM & © Warner Bros. Inc.

Ornament, plastic. Matrix Industries, Ltd., 1997. Tweety and Sylvester are shown singing Christmas carols. 4.25" tall. $25-40. TM & © Warner Bros. Inc.

Ornament, plastic. Matrix Industries, Ltd., 1997. Taz is shown in a box of popcorn. Caption: "Fresh popcorn." 3" tall. $20-35. TM & © Warner Bros. Inc.

Ornament, plastic. Matrix Industries, Ltd., 1997. Daffy Duck is shown driving a fire truck. 3" tall. $20-35. TM & © Warner Bros. Inc.

Ornament, plastic. Matrix Industries, Ltd., 1997. Bugs Bunny is shown on top of a director's board. Caption: "'Twas the Night before Christmas." 4" tall. $20-35. TM & © Warner Bros. Inc.

Ornament, plastic. Matrix Industries, Ltd., 1997. Sylvester is shown standing next to a gumball machine. Caption: "Happy holidays." 4.5" tall. $25-40. TM & © Warner Bros. Inc.

Ornament, plastic. Matrix Industries, Ltd., 1997. Taz is shown coming out of a trunk filled with ornaments. 3" tall. $20-35. TM & © Warner Bros. Inc.

Ornament, plastic. Matrix Industries, Ltd., 1997. Daffy Duck is shown dropping presents out of an airplane. 4" tall. $20-35. TM & © Warner Bros. Inc.

Ornament, plastic. Matrix Industries, Ltd., 1997. Tweety is shown standing on the fireplace mantle. 3.5" tall. $20-35. TM & © Warner Bros. Inc.

Ornament, plastic. Matrix Industries, Ltd., 1997. Taz is shown in a cookie jar. 3.5" tall. $20-35. TM & © Warner Bros. Inc.

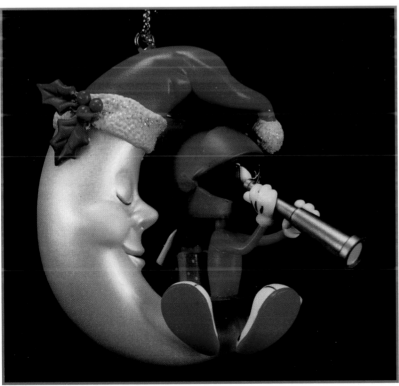

Ornament, plastic. Matrix Industries, Ltd., 1997. Marvin the Martian is shown on the moon. 3" tall. $20-35. TM & © Warner Bros. Inc.

Ornament, plastic. Matrix Industries, Ltd., 1997. Road Runner is shown standing on top of candy cane striped dynamite. 3.5" tall. $25-40. TM & © Warner Bros. Inc.

Ornament, plastic. Matrix Industries, Ltd., 1997. Sylvester and Tweety are shown on a cookie jar. Caption: "Homemade cookies." 3.5" tall. $25-40. TM & © Warner Bros. Inc.

Ornament, plastic. Matrix Industries, Ltd.,
1997. She-devil is shown playing the piano.
3" tall. $25-40. TM & © Warner Bros. Inc.

Ornament, plastic. Matrix Industries, Ltd.,
1997. Bugs Bunny is shown golfing. 4" tall.
Caption: "Happy holidays." $20-35. TM & ©
Warner Bros. Inc.

Ornament, plastic. Matrix Industries, Ltd., 1997. Taz is sitting in a grocery basket. 2.75" tall. $20-35. TM & © Warner Bros. Inc.

Ornament, plastic. Matrix Industries, Ltd., 1997. Tweety is shown on top of a camera. 3" tall. $20-35. TM & © Warner Bros. Inc.

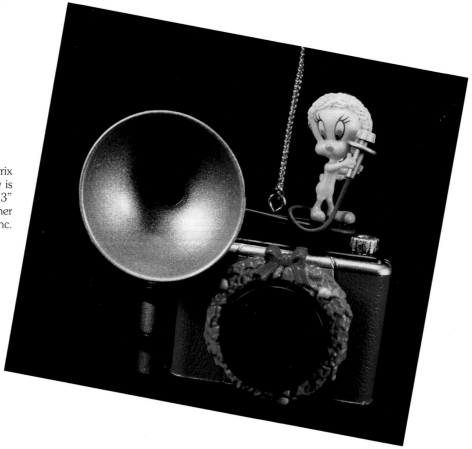

Display, plastic/fabric. Matrix Industries, Ltd., 1997. Animated. Taz is shown eating a gift wrapped present. 18.5" tall. $75-90. TM & © Warner Bros. Inc.

Display, plastic/fabric. Matrix Industries, Ltd., 1997. Animated. Sylvester is shown holding a candle. 22.5" tall. $75-90. TM & © Warner Bros. Inc.

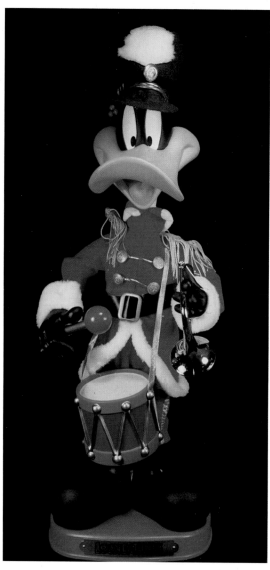

Display, plastic/fabric. Matrix Industries,
Ltd.,1997. Animated. Daffy Duck is shown
dressed as a solider. 24" tall. $75-90. TM &
© Warner Bros. Inc.

Display, plastic/fabric. Matrix Industries,
Ltd, 1997. Animated. Taz is shown
dressed like a chef. 17.5" tall. $75-90.
TM & © Warner Bros. Inc.

Display, plastic/fabric. Matrix Industries, Ltd., 1996. Animated. Bugs Bunny is shown riding in a sleigh that Taz is pulling. Approximately 24" tall. $150-165. TM & © Warner Bros. Inc.

Display, plastic/fabric. Matrix Industries, Ltd., 1997. Animated. Bugs Bunny is shown dressed as Santa. $75-90. TM & © Warner Bros. Inc.

Bibliography

Beck, Jerry, and Friedwald, Will. *Warner Bros. Animation Art. The Characters. The Creators. The Limited Editions.* Warner Bros. Worldwide Publishing, 1997.

Korbeck, Sharon. *Toy Shop* magazine. Iola, Wisconsin: Krause Publications, Bi-weekly distribution 1998.

Pope, Gail, and Hammond, Keith. *Fast Food Toys.* Atglen, Pennsylvania: Schiffer Publishing, Ltd., 1996.

Soloman, Charles. *The History of Animation. Enchanted Drawings.* Avenel, New Jersey: Wong books-distributed by Random House Value Publishing, Inc., 1989, 1994.

Woodall, Allen, and Brickell, Sean. *The Illustrated Encyclopedia of Metal Lunch Boxes.* West Chester, Pennsylvania: Schiffer Publishing, Ltd., 1992.

http://wbstore.com

http://www.cerbslair.com/ltcc/ltnews.html